Inspiration® in Science

Science and Society

Life Science

Physical Science

Earth Science

7412 SW Beaverton Hillsdale Hwy, Ste. 102
Portland, OR 97225-2167 USA

Phone: 503-297-3004
Fax: 503-297-4676
www.inspiration.com

Inspiration®
SOFTWARE, INC

Publisher: Mona L. Westhaver

Author: Bob Madar

Editor: Jonathan Maier

Associate Editor: Linnea Johnsson

Layout/Design: Christine Washburn

Introduction

Dear educator,

Learning to think. Learning to learn. These are the essential skills for student success in every curriculum area and academic pursuit. Research in educational theory and cognitive psychology tells us that visual learning techniques—ways of working with information and presenting ideas graphically—are among the very best methods for teaching students of all ages how to think and how to learn. Working visually inspires students to tap into creative thinking, and to clarify their thoughts, reinforce understanding, integrate new knowledge, and identify misconceptions.

Inspiration® in Science is designed to help educators integrate visual learning into their science curriculum. Focused on standards derived from individual states and professional organizations, each lesson ties curriculum and visual learning together to help you improve your students' academic achievement.

This book is just a start. We hope these lesson plans will stimulate your own creativity as you adapt them to the needs, contexts, and learning styles of your students. Most importantly, we hope that the learning strategies presented here will serve your students throughout their education and provide a foundation for lifelong learning.

Mona L. Westhaver

Mona L. Westhaver
President and Co-founder
Inspiration Software, Inc.

About *Inspiration® in Science*

Organization

The major sections of *Inspiration® in Science* reflect those found in state and national standards: Science and Society, Life Science, Physical Science, and Earth Science. Within each section, lessons are designated middle school or high school. You may find it helpful to review lessons from subjects and grade levels outside your area; many lessons can easily be modified for other content and classrooms. Additional sections at the end of the book offer further resources for curriculum development and enrichment.

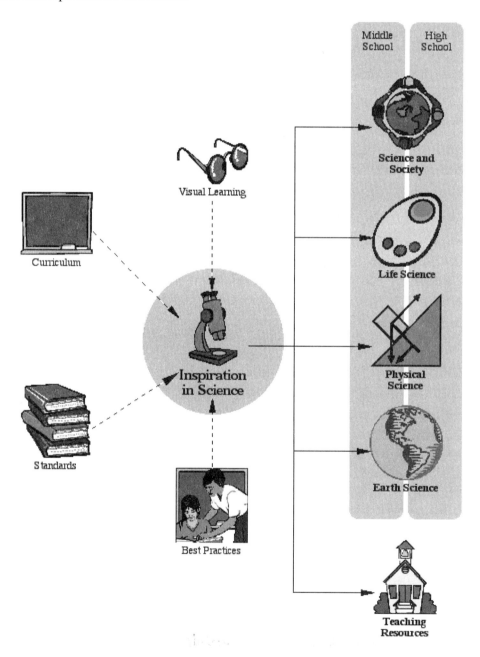

Downloadable templates

Many of the Inspiration templates and examples found throughout this book were designed specifically for these lessons. These valuable and time-saving resources can be easily downloaded at www.inspiration.com/inscience. Please note: If a template is mentioned without reference to downloading, then it is already available in Inspiration by selecting the Open Template command on the File menu.

Get inspired!

We hope this book inspires you to make the lessons your own: mold them to match your teaching style and the needs of your students. Feel free to contact us with your questions, insights, and great ideas! We love to hear from educators!

Table of Contents

Science and Society

Inventions: Science for Society

Overview

Science and technology have a dynamic relationship. Scientific discoveries make technological innovations possible which, in turn, lead to new scientific knowledge. In this project, students use basic science to design tools to assist students with disabilities in the laboratory.

Standard

Students apply science knowledge and skills to solve problems or meet challenges.

Materials needed

Informational material on physical disabilities and their causes, and examples of prosthetic devices

Preparation

1. Download the following Invention Solutions template at www.inspiration.com/inscience or create your own version and save it using the Inspiration® Template Wizard.

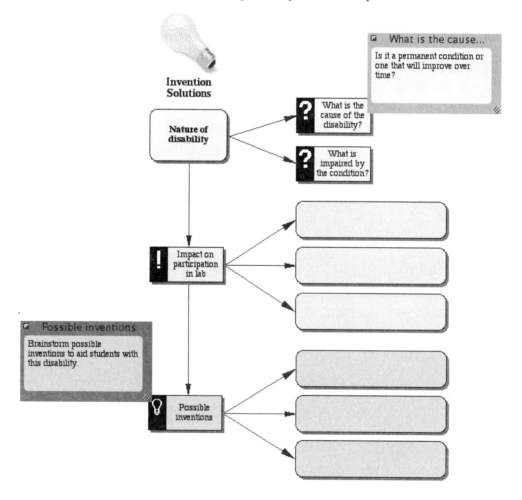

2. Invite an expert, such as an occupational therapist from your school district, to give students a presentation on physical disabilities and the specific challenges faced by students with these conditions.

3. As a class, brainstorm a list of physical disabilities that could benefit from an invention. Use the RapidFire® tool to record student ideas.

Lesson

1. Group students into teams of four to research one of the physical disabilities they identified in the brainstorming session.

2. Ask teams to propose inventions that allow students with the disability to more fully participate in laboratory activities. Encourage teams to record research and invention ideas in the Invention Solutions template.

3. As a class, create a list of criteria for the inventions, such as portability, ease of use, cost of construction, purchase price, and size.

4. Have each team use Inspiration to plan and design an assistive invention that addresses all the criteria.

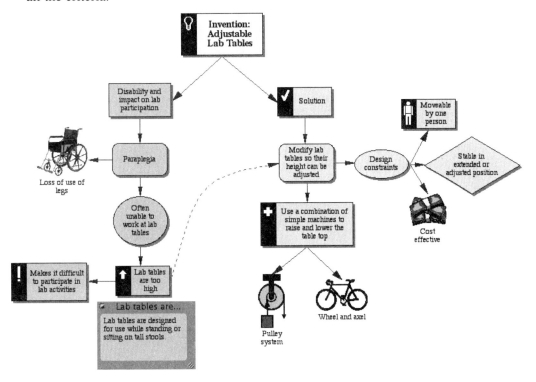

5. Invite teams to present their invention diagrams to the class. Ask the expert who presented earlier to attend and participate in the evaluation of each team's work.

Technology Over Time

Overview

Human solutions to practical problems often use scientific knowledge to develop new technologies. In this lesson, students recognize the importance of scientific discoveries to human welfare by researching a technological innovation.

Standard

Students know that throughout history diverse cultures developed scientific ideas and solved human problems through technology.

Materials needed

Informational material on the history of technology

Preparation

1. Ask students to form teams of four and generate a list of basic human needs.

2. Have teams share their thoughts with the rest of the class. Open a new Inspiration® diagram and use the RapidFire® tool to record their ideas for future reference.

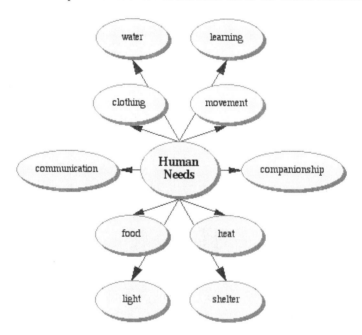

Lesson

1. Ask each team to select one of the human needs suggested by the class and identify a technological innovation that helps people meet this need.

2. Have teams research the history of their innovation's development. Provide them with criteria to guide research, such as need for the technology, science behind the innovation, commercial applications, and impact on older technologies.

3. As teams conduct their research, instruct them to capture the information they gather in a diagram. Encourage them to add details using the Note tool.

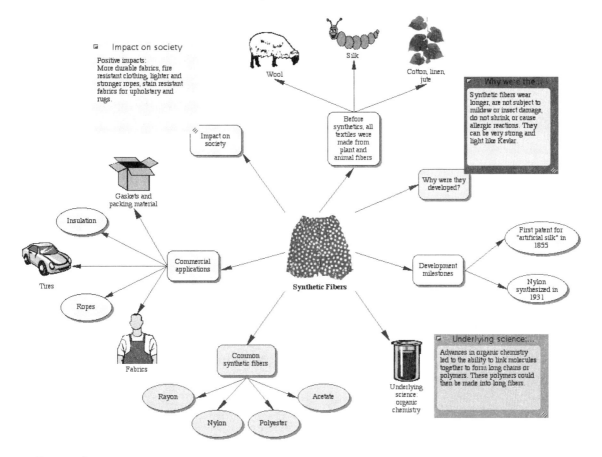

Extension

Have teams revisit the human need they selected earlier and research various ways in which this need has been met by different cultures throughout time. Tell them to create a diagram that charts the progression of technological innovations that have addressed this need.

Life Science

Tree Identification Key

Overview

Dichotomous keys are widely used in the biological sciences to identify and classify organisms. In this lesson, students develop a classification system for an assortment of tree leaves and use this system to create a dichotomous key to identify trees at a local site.

Standard

Students understand that living things are classified by internal and external features.

Materials needed

- From a local open space, such as a park or school grounds, a collection of various types of tree branches with attached leaves
- Handouts with a list of terminology covering basic leaf anatomy
- Hand lenses or dissecting microscopes
- Examples of dichotomous keys

Preparation

1. Label each type of branch with the common name of the tree from which it came.

2. Download the following Leaf Morphology template at www.inspiration.com/inscience or create your own version and save it using the Inspiration® Template Wizard.

Leaf Morphology
- I. Leaf type: Needle
  - A. Tree name:
    1. Arrangement on stem:
    2. Attachment:
  - B. Tree name:
    1. Arrangement on stem:
    2. Attachment:
  - C. Tree name:
    1. Arrangement on stem:
    2. Attachment:
- II. Leaf type: Broad leaf
  - A. Tree name:
    1. Arrangement on stem:
    2. Attachment:
    3. Veination pattern:
    4. Leaf margins:

Lesson

1. Have students form teams of four and provide each team with branches from three different tree species.

2. Ask students to write down aspects of leaf structure, attachment, and arrangement they could use to classify the leaves. Have two or three teams meet and discuss their ideas.

3. Distribute the leaf terminology handouts and ask individual teams to compare their ideas with the list of accepted terms.

4. Discuss with students the necessity of a universally accepted set of terms for classifying living things.

5. Provide the teams with branches from each tree species at the site.

6. Instruct teams to open the Leaf Morphology template and, for each species, enter their observations into the appropriate topic.

7. Distribute the examples of dichotomous keys to teams for examination. Explain the structure of a dichotomous key.

8. Instruct teams to use the information in their Leaf Morphology outlines to create a dichotomous key diagram for identifying trees at the site.

Extension

Invite an elementary class to the studied site and have the teams help small groups of elementary students use the dichotomous keys to identify the trees.

Creating a Family Pedigree

Overview

Charting the presence or absence of certain easily observable traits helps students understand basic concepts of heredity and Mendelian genetics. In this lesson, students use Inspiration® to create a pedigree of a particular trait for three generations of a family.

Standards

• Students design and conduct scientific investigations.

• Students know one or more genes can determine an inherited trait.

Preparation

1. Download the following Class Trait Distribution template at www.inspiration.com/inscience or create your own version and save it using the Inspiration Template Wizard.

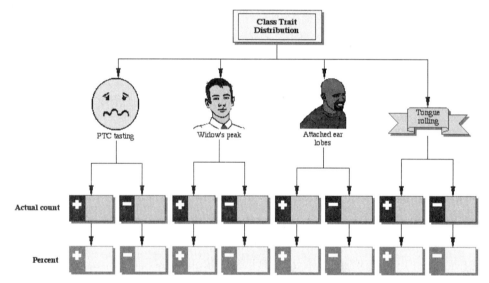

2. You may find it useful to download the Family Pedigree example at www.inspiration.com/inscience.

3. Review with students principles of basic genetics, in particular, dominant and recessive alleles, the relationship between genotype and phenotype, and the law of independent assortment.

Lesson

1. Have students open the Class Trait Distribution template. Poll the class to determine how many students carry each trait. Ask them to enter the number of classmates with and without each trait into the appropriate symbols.

2. Instruct students to calculate the percentage of the class that do and do not have each characteristic and enter those values into the appropriate symbols.

3. Ask students if they think the phenotypes they observe are the results of dominant or recessive allele and why they think that is the case.

4. Inform students they will construct a three-generation family pedigree for one of the traits. Advise them to select a trait they can successfully research. For example, students who do not have easy access to all three generations should not choose the ability to taste PTC (phenylthiocarbamide).

5. Instruct students to start with a list of all known relatives, recording the year of their birth, relationship to the student, and presence or absence of the trait.

6. Review the following elements of a family pedigree diagram with your students:

- Females are represented by circles and males by rectangles.
- Filled in circles and squares indicate that the person has that trait.
- Straight horizontal lines connecting two people indicate a union.
- Vertical lines represent offspring.
- Roman numerals represent generations.

7. Have students create their family pedigree diagram. As a starting point, they may find it helpful to use the Family Pedigree example you downloaded earlier.

8. Ask students to form teams in which each member has studied a different trait.

9. Have students compare their pedigrees within the team and determine which of the traits represent a dominant or a recessive allele.

The Cell as Factory

Overview

Cells are highly structured, complex systems that perform a wide variety of functions. In this lesson, students compare the operations of a cell to those of a manufacturing plant. This analogy is useful for understanding the contributions made by cellular organelles to the overall functioning of a cell.

Standard

Students know the basic components and functions of cells.

Materials needed

- Informational material on factory operations, including a description of a local manufacturing company if possible

- Informational material on cell structure and function

Preparation

Download the following Cell as Factory template at www.inspiration.com/inscience or create your own version and save it using the Inspiration® Template Wizard.

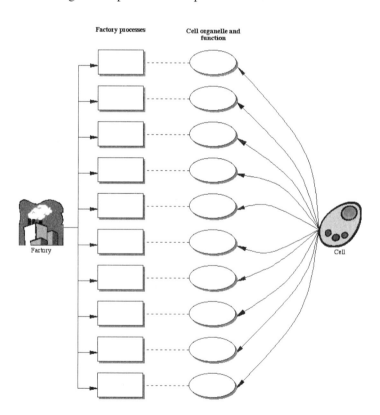

Lesson

1. Ask students to consult the informational material on factory operations. With a partner, have them develop a list of processes necessary for a factory to function.

2. Ask students to share their lists with the class. Record their ideas in a diagram using the RapidFire® tool. Save the diagram for students to reference later.

3. Provide students with the informational material on cell structure and function. Ask them to note passages describing the processes necessary for a cell to function and the organelles responsible for carrying out these functions.

4. Have students open the Cell as Factory template and use it to record factory functions and analogous cell functions. Encourage students to revisit informational materials for additional cell or factory functions that may help them complete the template.

Biome Comparison Study

Overview

Comparing different biomes builds understanding of ecosystem dynamics and the interplay of abiotic and biotic components. In this lesson, students investigate a biome and compare their findings with fellow students.

Standard

Students know factors that affect the number and types of organisms an ecosystem can support.

Materials needed

- Informational material on biomes, such as the NASA biome research web site, http://earthobservatory.nasa.gov/Laboratory/Biome/

- Tape and scissors for each team of students

Preparation

Download the following Biome template at www.inspiration.com/inscience or create your own version and save it using the Inspiration® Template Wizard.

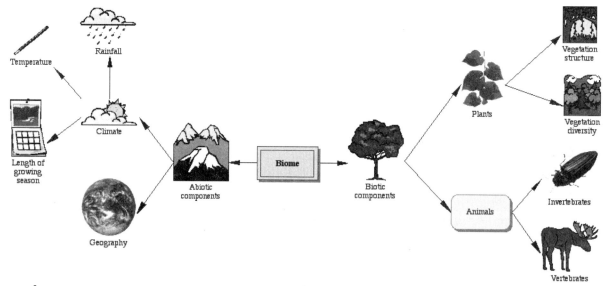

Lesson

1. Ask students to form teams of two or three and have them select a biome to research. Ensure that the full range of biomes is represented.

2. Instruct teams to research their biome using the provided informational material.

3. Have teams open the Biome template and record their findings. Encourage them to add symbols and notes as necessary.

4. Instruct teams to print their diagrams over six to nine pages to create a poster. To do so, use the Scale Diagram option found in the Page Setup dialog. Provide tape and scissors to teams and allow time for them to construct their posters.

5. Ask each team to meet with at least two other teams who have researched different biomes and compare their diagrams. Instruct them to speculate on the effect of abiotic components on the biotic components of the ecosystems.

6. Invite students to share their posters with the class. Lead a discussion on the interrelationship of abiotic and biotic components, referring to evidence displayed in the teams' diagrams.

The Food Web

Overview

Organisms are linked to one another by the transfer of matter and energy. By analyzing the trophic relationships in a biome, students increase their understanding of community ecology and the underlying relationships that bind living things together.

Standard

Students describe matter and energy flow in living systems.

Materials needed

• Examples of food web diagrams

• Informational material on biomes, such as the NASA biome research web site, http://earthobservatory.nasa.gov/Laboratory/Biome/

Preparation

1. Download the following Trophic Level Analysis template at www.inspiration.com/inscience or create your own version and save it using the Inspiration® Template Wizard.

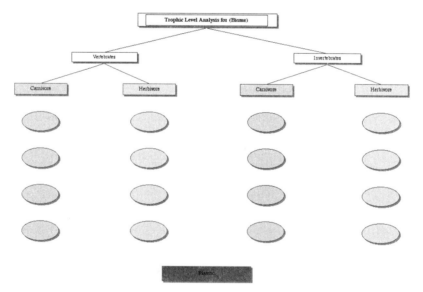

2. Review with students the principles of constructing food webs, referring to examples.

3. Review with students basic biological processes such as photosynthesis, respiration, herbivory, and predation.

Lesson

1. Ask students to select a biome and research the trophic relationships using the provided informational material. Ensure that the full range of biomes is represented.

2. Instruct students to open the Trophic Level Analysis template and record names of organisms in the appropriate symbols.

3. Have students use the Link tool to represent the feeding relationships between the organisms recorded in the symbols.

4. Instruct students to create a food web of their biome by modifying the Trophic Level Analysis diagram. Encourage them to replace the existing symbols with appropriate symbols from the Animals—Plants symbol libraries.

5. Have students share their food web diagrams.

6. Ask students to reflect on the statement, "A change in a plant can affect the largest predator." Engage them in a discussion on why this is the case, emphasizing the transfer of energy and matter through living systems.

DNA Fingerprinting

Overview

DNA fingerprinting is a result of recent advances in molecular genetics. The process makes it possible to match tissue, hair, or fluids to the person from whom they came. In this lesson, students use Inspiration® to organize research on DNA fingerprinting into an informational pamphlet.

Standard

Students understand that the level of relatedness between organisms can be measured by comparing the similarity of their DNA sequences.

Materials needed

• Informational material on molecular genetics and DNA fingerprinting technologies, including the potential misuse of DNA fingerprinting techniques

• Case studies on the use of DNA fingerprinting in solving criminal cases and diagnosing genetic diseases

Preparation

1. Ask students to form teams of four and select one member as the recorder.

2. Have each team discuss what they know about DNA fingerprinting. Encourage teams to identify gaps in their knowledge and develop a list of questions about the technology and its uses.

3. Invite teams to present their questions to the class. Use the RapidFire® tool to record the questions in an Inspiration diagram. Save this diagram for student reference.

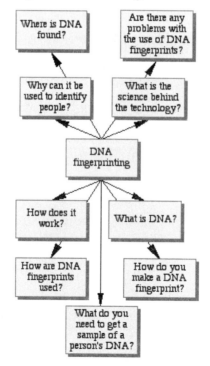

Lesson

1. Instruct teams to research aspects of DNA fingerprinting, such as the basic techniques involved, benefits and drawbacks of its use, and case studies. Ask them to record their findings in a diagram like the one below. Have them use the Note tool to record details.

2. Ask teams to present their diagrams to the class and encourage discussion. During the presentations, check for accuracy of information and help students clarify any misunderstandings.

3. Instruct teams to revise their diagrams based on the class discussion.

4. Have teams switch to Outline View and edit their information to form the foundation of an informative pamphlet on the pros and cons of DNA fingerprinting.

5. Instruct teams to click the Transfer button to finalize the layout of their pamphlet in a word processor.

6. Have teams copy their pamphlets and make them available to visitors during an open house.

Protein Synthesis

Overview

The study of protein synthesis sheds light on the central role of DNA in all living things. In this lesson, students research the process of protein synthesis and create a concept map based on their findings.

Standard

Students know the role of DNA in heredity and protein synthesis.

Materials needed

Informational material on the process of protein synthesis

Preparation

1. Review with students the structure of DNA and the nature of the genetic code.

2. Discuss with students the principles and components of a concept map.

Lesson

1. Have students form teams of two and consult the informational material on the process of protein synthesis.

2. Instruct teams to open the Inspiration® Science—Concept Map template and construct a concept map that diagrams the process of protein synthesis. Encourage teams to use the Note tool to record more detailed information.

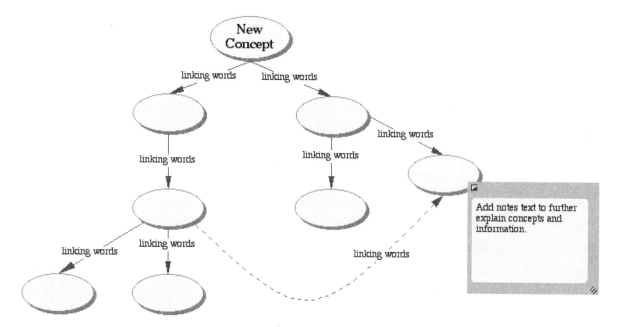

3. Have teams present their concept maps to the class. Invite students to ask clarifying questions and offer suggestions for revising and improving the maps.

4. Ask teams to revise their diagrams based on class feedback.

Extension

Have teams present their concept maps to students in a health education class studying genetic diseases. Encourage teams to note that genetic mutations are expressed through the process of protein synthesis.

Aquatic Pollution Study

Overview

Human activities have profound impact on natural systems. In this lesson, students use Inspiration® to design and implement an experiment testing the effects of common household chemicals on a model aquatic ecosystem.

Standards

- Students know ways in which humans can alter the equilibrium in ecosystems, causing irreversible effects.
- Students design and conduct scientific investigations.

Materials needed

- Informational material that outlines the ways common household chemicals, such as engine oil or anti-freeze, can negatively impact aquatic habitats
- Culture containers, such as small aquariums or quart-sized wide mouth canning jars
- Growing plant material from a pond habitat
- Bottled spring water
- Micropipettes
- Microscope slides and cover slips
- 3% methyl cellulose solution
- Compound microscopes
- Pollutants, such as engine oil or chlorine bleach

Preparation

1. Review with students the ecology and life history of ciliates such as paramecium.

2. Review with students principles of experimental design, such as the need for replication and the importance of a control group.

3. Provide students with the informational material on household chemicals.

Lesson

1. Ask students to form teams of two. Have them open the Inspiration Science—Experimental Design template and use it to design an experiment to test the impact of common household chemicals on aquatic habitats using the provided materials. Encourage teams to add notes and symbols as needed.

2. As the teams work on their designs, circulate and check for understanding and thoroughness.

3. Ask four teams to group together and discuss their work, revising their designs as needed.

4. Have teams discuss their designs with you prior to checking out the equipment necessary for the experiment.

5. As the teams conduct the experiments, monitor their progress and check to make sure they follow proper laboratory procedure.

Continued next page

6. Once the experiments are completed and the teams have analyzed their data, instruct them to open their Experimental Design diagram and switch to Outline View. Ask teams to add their results and conclusions to their outlines using the Topic tool.

Experimental Design

I. Purpose
To test the effect of anti-freeze on aquatic ecosystems

II. Hypothesis
Addition of anti-freeze to model aquatic ecosystems will depress ciliate populations. The negative effect on the ciliate populations will be directly proportional to the concentration of anti-freeze in the system.

III. Method

   A. Step 1
   Select and sterilize five wide mouth canning jars.

   B. Step 2
   To each of the four jars add 700 ml of bottled spring water and 20 gm of plant material collected from a local pond.

   C. Step 3
   Measure out 10 ml, 15 ml, 20 ml, and 25 ml samples of anti-freeze and randomly assign one sample to one of the four jars. Label the experimental jars with their respective treatment. The fifth jar will serve as the control.

   D. Step 4
   Allow the jars to sit on a lab bench at room temperature for eight days.

   E. Step 5
   Use the micropipette to sample the ciliate population at a depth of 2 mm below the water surface. Add one drop of the sample to a glass microscope slide, add a drop of 3% methyl cellulose and a cover slip and count the number of ciliates present at a magnification of 100X. Repeat this process five times for each treatment and the control.

   F. Step 6
   Place the contents of the treatment jars in a suitable waste container and wash the jars, pipettes, and slides.

IV. Materials
List necessary materials and equipment.

   A. Five quart-sized wide mouth canning jars

   B. Aquatic plant material

   C. Bottled spring water

   D. 50 ml and 1000 ml graduated cylinders

   E. Micropipettes

   F. Microscope slides and cover slips

   G. 3% methyl cellulose solution

   H. Compound microscopes

   I. Anti-freeze

V. Data

   A. Analysis
   Counts will be averaged, and analyzed in a bar graph format.

   B. Data format
   The data table will be formatted so that each count can be entered into a cell associated with either a specific treatment or the control.

7. Have students click the Transfer button to finalize their lab report in a
word processor.

Extension
Instruct students to inventory the types of chemicals present in their homes, and report how to
manage the disposal of the chemicals to minimize negative impacts on local aquatic ecosystems.

Constructing a Cladogram

Overview

Organisms descended from a common ancestor share features inherited from that ancestor. Biologists use these similarities to classify organisms. In this lesson, students research morphological features shared by different groups of vertebrates, and construct a cladogram representing the major trends of vertebrate phylogeny.

Standard

Students are able to analyze relationships among organisms and develop a model of a hierarchical classification system based on similarities and differences.

Materials needed

Informational material on the morphology of the major vertebrate divisions

Preparation

Download the following Cladogram template at www.inspiration.com/inscience or create your own version and save it using the Inspiration® Template Wizard.

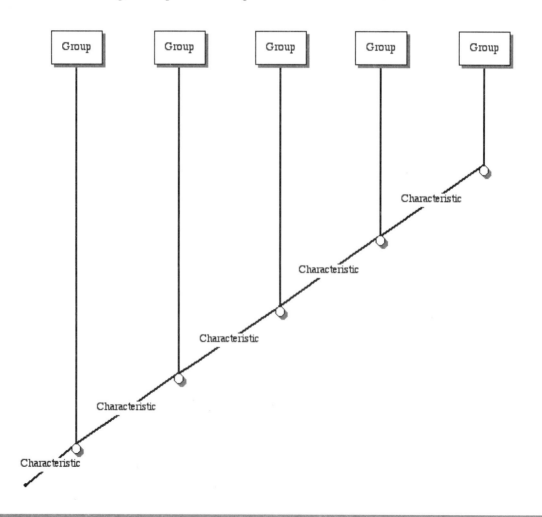

Lesson

1. Ask students to form teams of two or three. Instruct them to consult the informational material on morphology and identify the major morphological differences of the various classes of vertebrates.

2. Have them open a new Inspiration document and switch to Outline View to record their findings.

3. Discuss with the class the principles and components of a cladogram.

4. Instruct teams to open the Cladogram template. Have them consult the information in their outlines in order to construct a cladogram of the major vertebrate groups.

5. Ask the class to form groups of three teams each to compare and discuss their cladograms.

6. It is likely that there will be some difference of opinion about which characteristics are the most important in separating out the major vertebrate groups. Engage the class in a general discussion on the difficulty of selecting classification characteristics that effectively delineate the evolutionary relationships between organisms.

Physical Science

States of Matter

Overview

In this lesson, students hypothesize on the behavior of solids, liquids, and gases and design experiments to test their predictions. Students combine the results of their experiments with research to create a presentation on the states of matter.

Standards

• Students design and conduct scientific investigations.

• Students know that the states of matter depend on molecular arrangement and motion.

Materials needed

• Internet sites and other informational material on the states of matter

• Materials and equipment necessary for conducting demonstrations on the states of matter (for example, liquid nitrogen, dry ice, and a Cartesian Diver)

• Lab equipment and materials to conduct states of matter experiments

Lesson

1. Present demonstrations on the behavior of various states of matter for the class. Ask students to note their observations.

2. Have students form teams of three or four and discuss what they observed.

3. Ask each team to develop a list of questions about the states of matter and how matter changes from one state to another.

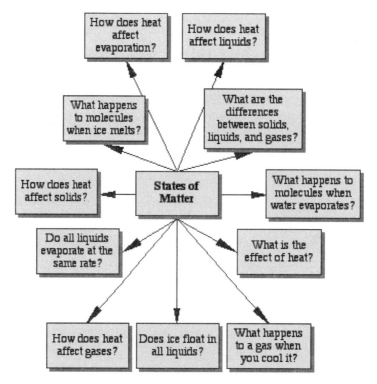

4. Invite teams to share their questions with the class. Record questions in an Inspiration® diagram using the RapidFire® tool.

5. Help students identify which of the questions can be investigated with the available lab equipment.

6. Ask each team to select one of these questions, guiding their decisions so all states of matter are represented.

7. Instruct each team to open the Science—Experimental Design template and use it to design an experiment that addresses their question. Encourage them to add notes and symbols as needed.

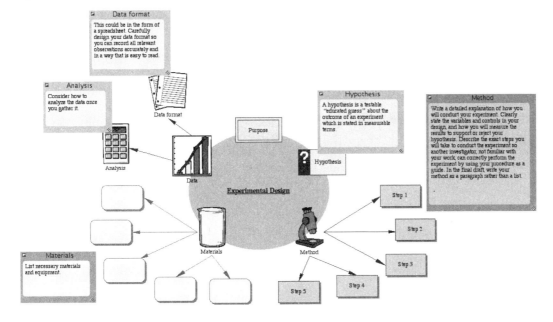

8. As teams work on their designs, circulate and check for understanding and thoroughness.

9. Have teams discuss their designs with you prior to checking out the equipment and materials necessary for the experiment.

Continued next page

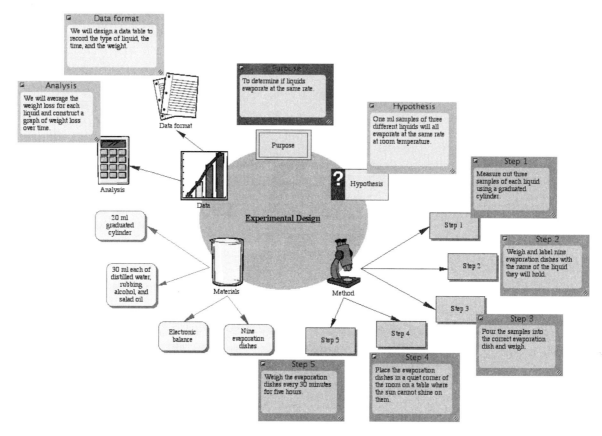

10. After teams complete their experiments, ask students to form new teams in which each member has performed an experiment on a different state of matter.

11. Have teams consult the provided Internet sites and informational material to research the physics underlying the states of matter, such as the effect of heat energy on molecular motion, and attractive forces between molecules.

12. Instruct teams to reference their research and experimental findings to create a diagram on the three states of matter. Encourage them to use the Hyperlink tool to connect the appropriate text to supporting documents (for example, a spreadsheet of their data or a web site showing a simulation of the arrangement of molecules in a solid).

13. Have teams present their diagrams to the class. Encourage students to look for underlying principles of the states of matter and guide them to an understanding of the kinetic theory of matter.

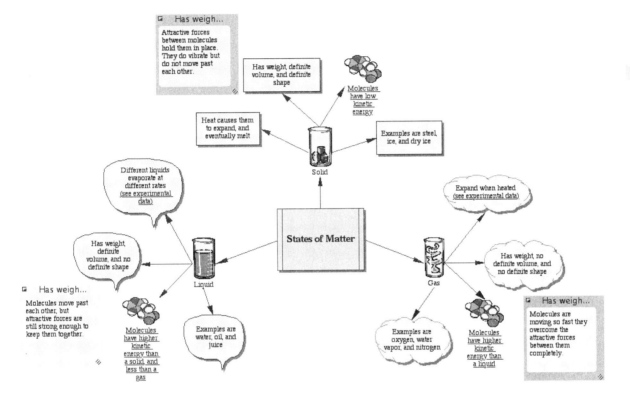

Chemical and Physical Changes

Overview

In this lesson, students conduct several lab activities that help them identify, compare, and understand physical and chemical changes. Students use Inspiration® to record and classify their findings.

Standard

Students are expected to distinguish between physical and chemical changes in matter.

Materials needed

• A complete range of chemical and physical change lab activities

• Informational material on the nature of chemical and physical changes

Preparation

1. Download the following Chemical and Physical Change template at www.inspiration.com/inscience or create your own version and save it using the Inspiration Template Wizard.

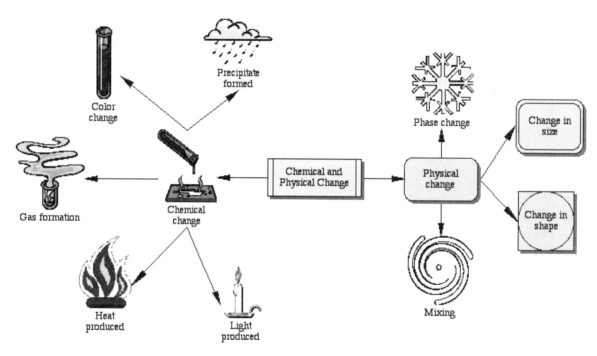

2. Set up lab activity stations that demonstrate each type of chemical and physical change identified in the template.

Lesson

1. Have students form teams of three or four and ask them to perform the experiments at each lab station.

2. Encourage students to take notes on the outcome of each experiment.

3. Instruct teams to open the Chemical and Physical Change template and use the Note tool to enter experiment names into notes attached to the appropriate symbols.

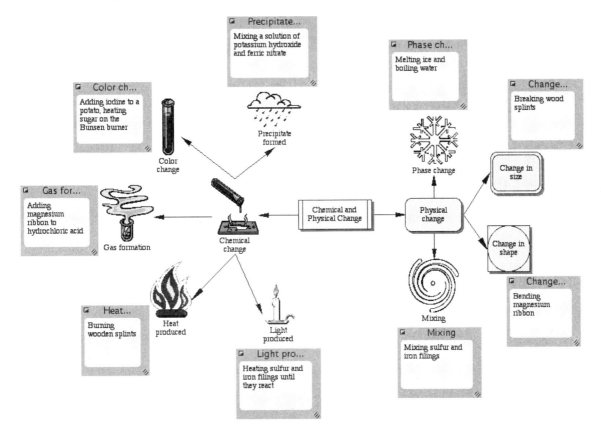

4. Instruct teams to submit their diagrams for review. Check their work for misconceptions or inaccuracies. Follow up with a class discussion to clarify understanding.

The Physics of Motion

Overview

In this lesson, students build devices in which a marble travels, beginning to end, for one minute. They gain insight into the physics of motion by analyzing their devices in an Inspiration® diagram.

Standard

Students understand the components of motion such as speed, acceleration, and velocity.

Materials needed

- Informational material on the physics of motion
- Stopwatches
- Flat pieces of cardboard, at least 25 cm x 50 cm
- Used file folders
- Masking tape
- Marbles

Preparation

Download the following Marble Motion Analysis template at www.inspiration.com/inscience or create your own version and save it using the Inspiration Template Wizard.

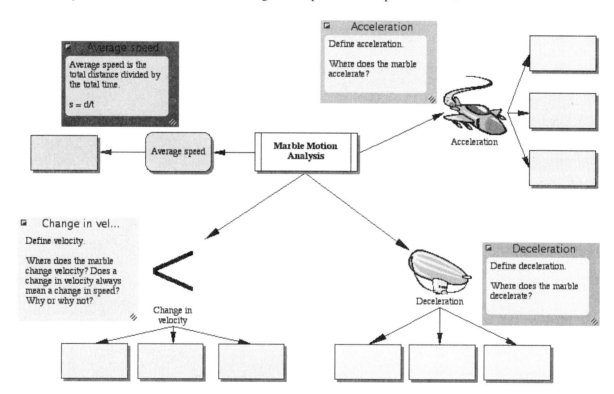

Lesson

1. Ask students to form teams of three and provide each team with cardboard, file folders, masking tape, a stopwatch, and marbles.

2. Using the material provided, instruct each team to build a device in which a marble travels, beginning to end, for exactly one minute. Travel time is to be measured from the instant of the marble's release to when it makes contact with the floor. Teams cannot push the marble when it is released or touch the marble once it is in motion.

3. As teams finalize their devices, encourage them to confirm the consistency of the travel time with multiple runs.

4. Ask each team to present its device to the class. Tell students to pay close attention to points at which marbles change speed and direction.

5. Lead the class in a discussion on the formal definitions of acceleration, deceleration, and velocity. Solicit examples of these terms from observations made about the devices. For student reference, provide informational material on the physics of motion.

6. Have students return to their original teams. Instruct each team to open the Marble Motion Analysis template and enter information on their device into the appropriate symbols and notes.

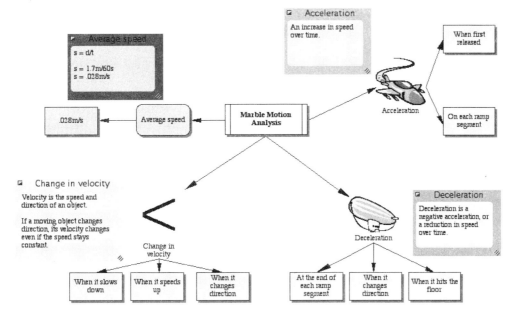

7. Instruct each student to write a paragraph that applies the physics of motion to a type of transportation with which they have firsthand experience (for example, a bicycle or skateboard).

Pendulum Investigation

Overview

Investigating the behavior of a simple pendulum builds student understanding of energy transfer, motion, and momentum. In this lesson, students engage in scientific inquiry and design a device with an oscillation period of one second.

Standards

- Students develop the necessary abilities to perform scientific inquiry.
- Students develop an understanding of motion, forces, and the transfer of energy.

Materials needed

- One setup per team:

    - Ring stand and ring

    - 50 cm piece of string or fishing line

    - Assorted weights, such as washers or fishing weights

    - Stopwatch

Preparation

Review with students such concepts as gravitational force, potential energy, and kinetic energy.

Lesson

1. Demonstrate the action of a pendulum to the class, pointing out the pivot point and the bob. Tell them the period of a pendulum is the time required for a complete back and forth cycle.

2. Ask the class to brainstorm what conditions they could change to either lengthen or shorten the period of the pendulum. Record their ideas in an Inspiration® diagram using the RapidFire® tool. Save the diagram for student reference.

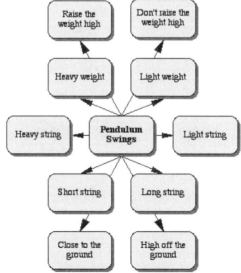

3. Ask students to form teams of three or four and have them design a pendulum with a period of one second.

4. Refer teams to the brainstorm diagram and ask them to predict how implementing the suggestions recorded in the diagram will affect the period of the pendulum.

5. Instruct the teams to identify where in the pendulum's cycle the following occur:

- Potential energy is at a maximum or a minimum.
- Kinetic energy is at a maximum or a minimum.
- Velocity of the bob is at a maximum or a minimum.
- The bob is accelerating or decelerating.

6. Ask teams to create a diagram that illustrates their conclusions about the motion of a pendulum.

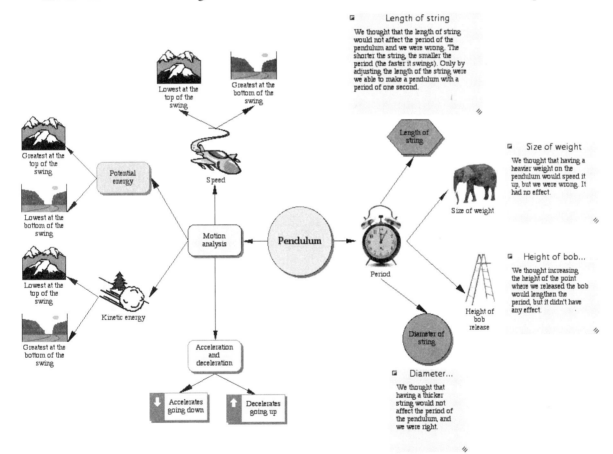

7. Encourage teams to share their diagrams with at least two other teams and elicit feedback. Have teams revise their diagrams as necessary.

Newton's Laws: Sports Analysis

Overview

Newton's three laws of motion are fundamental to understanding the behavior of moving bodies. In this lesson, students apply their knowledge of these laws to analyze various motions found in sports.

Standard

Students know that Newton's laws predict the motion of most objects.

Preparation

Review with students Newton's laws of motion.

Lesson

1. Instruct students to form teams of three or four and choose a familiar sport to investigate. Guide their selections so a variety of sports are represented.

2. Ask each team to open a new Inspiration® diagram. Using the RapidFire® tool, have them brainstorm examples of the types of motion found in their sport.

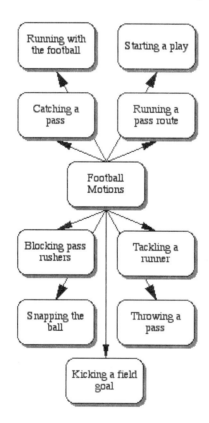

3. Instruct teams to analyze and discuss which of Newton's laws best explains the types of motion they identified.

4. Have teams modify and develop their brainstorm diagram to illustrate their conclusions.

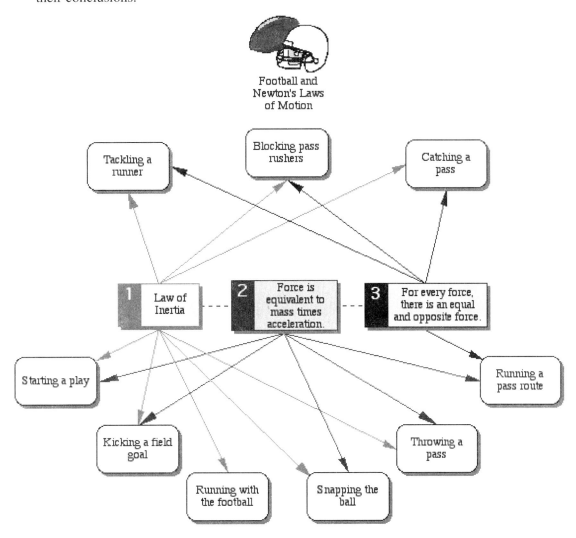

5. Ask teams to present their diagrams to the class. Encourage students to question each team's rationale for deciding which of Newton's laws best explain the motions they analyzed.

6. Have teams revise their diagrams based on class feedback.

Thermodynamics of Internal Combustion Engines

Overview

In this lesson, students demonstrate their knowledge of the laws of thermodynamics by analyzing the role of those laws in the operation of an internal combustion engine.

Standards

- Students know that heat flow and work are two forms of energy transfer between systems.
- Students know that the work done by a heat engine is the difference between the heat flow into the engine at high temperature and the heat flow out at a lower temperature.

Materials needed

Informational material on the operation of internal combustion engines

Preparation

1. Contact a guest speaker to present on internal combustion engine operation. A local technical education program would be a good source for a speaker.

2. Review with students the first and second laws of thermodynamics.

3. Have students form teams of three or four and ask each team to list what they know about diesel and gasoline powered engines.

4. Ask teams to identify gaps in their knowledge and develop a list of questions about internal combustion engines.

5. Invite the teams to share their questions with the class and record them in an Inspiration® diagram using the RapidFire® tool. Provide a copy of the diagram to the guest speaker in advance of his or her presentation.

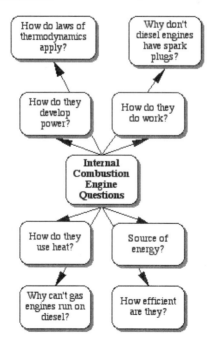

Lesson

1. Invite the guest speaker to discuss the operation of internal combustion engines with the class. Ask him or her to address the list of student questions during the course of the presentation.

2. In teams of four or five, have students construct a concept map that illustrates the role of thermodynamics in the operation of an internal combustion engine. Encourage teams to consult the informational material on internal combustion engines as necessary.

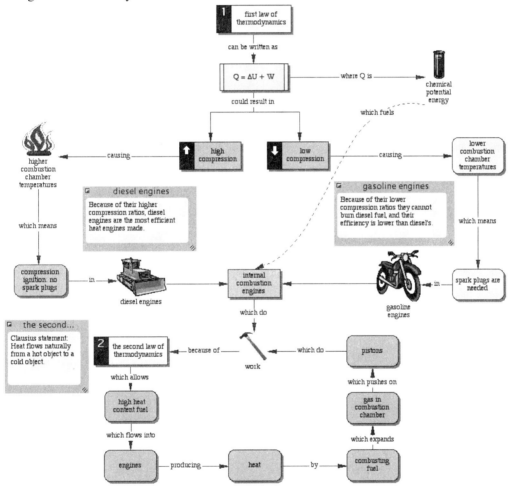

3. Have teams present their concept maps to the class. Invite students to ask clarifying questions and offer suggestions for improvement.

4. Ask teams to revise their concept maps based on the class feedback.

Extension

Encourage students to present their concept maps to the guest speaker. Ask him or her to comment on the clarity and accuracy of the presentations.

History of Physics

Overview

Studying the history of physics reveals how scientific knowledge grows and changes. In this lesson, students research important historical developments in physics and create a web site based on their findings.

Standard

Students research and describe the history of physics.

Materials needed

Informational material on the history of physics

Preparation

1. Provide students with an overview of the history of physics in preparation for their research.

2. Download the following Physics Milestone template at www.inspiration.com/inscience or create your own version by modifying the Inspiration® Social Studies—Historical Episode template and save it using the Template Wizard.

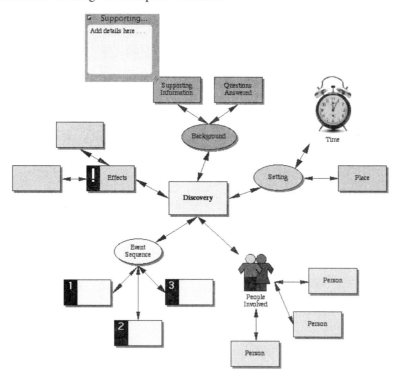

Lesson

1. Ask students to form teams of two and select an important historical development in physics to research.

2. Instruct teams to open the Physics Milestone template. Have them enter the results of their research into the appropriate symbols and add notes to record additional details. Remind them to use double-headed arrows for each link.

3. Ask teams to present their diagrams to the class. Have students check for accuracy and completeness of information. Encourage teams to revise their diagrams based on class feedback.

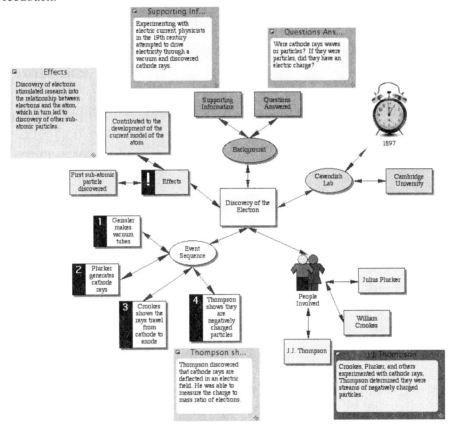

4. Assign one of the teams to develop the basis of a Milestones of Physics web site. Have them use the following procedure:

- Open a new diagram and enter "Milestones of Physics" into the symbol labeled "Main Idea."
- Select the Milestones of Physics symbol and use the Create tool to make linked symbols for each team's subject.
- Change all links to double-headed arrows using the Arrow Direction command on the Link menu.
- Use the Hyperlink tool to link each team's diagram to the appropriate symbol.
- Save the new diagram as Milestones of Physics.
- Export the diagram using the Export as HTML option on the File menu. Select the Site Skeleton® export to create the foundation of the web site.

5. Have teams use web site authoring software to finalize their web page designs.

DC Circuits

Overview

By designing and analyzing simple DC circuits, students gain a greater understanding of the basic principles of electricity and the laws which govern them. In this lesson, students use Inspiration® to model types of circuits prior to constructing and testing them in the laboratory.

Standards

• Students know how to predict the voltage or current in simple direct circuits.
• Students know how to solve problems involving Ohm's Law.

Materials needed

• DC power source (for example, a 9 Volt battery)

• Insulated wire of a suitable gauge

• Wire

• Single pole knife switches

• Assorted resistors or electric devices, such as low voltage lights, sockets, and buzzers

• Multimeter

Preparation

1. Review with students basic concepts of electricity, including Ohm's Law.

2. Instruct students in the use of the multimeter.

Lesson

1. Have students form teams of two. You may want to provide each team with a unique set of values for their circuit components.

2. Instruct teams to open a new Inspiration diagram and use the Science—Circuits symbol library to create a diagram of a DC circuit with resistors connected in series.

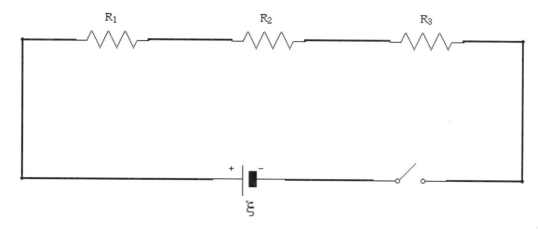

3. Have teams create a DC circuit diagram with resistors in parallel using the same components as in the series circuit.

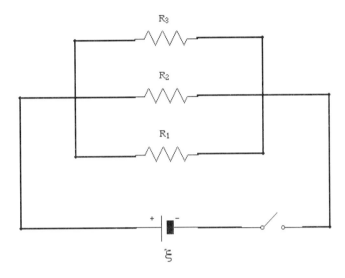

4. Instruct teams to design a circuit that contains two resistors in parallel connected to a third resistor in series.

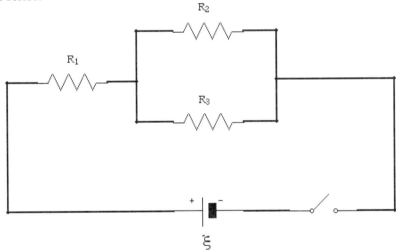

5. Have students use Ohm's Law to calculate the total resistance in each circuit, the current that flows through each resistor and through the circuit as a whole, and the voltage drop across each resistor.

6. Encourage each team to build the circuits they designed and check their calculations using the multimeter.

Visualizing Sound

Overview

Studying the physics of sound illuminates the characteristics and behavior of sound waves. In this lesson, students demonstrate their knowledge of sound waves by creating a concept map that includes audio samples.

Standard

Students know how to identify the characteristic properties of waves.

Materials needed

• Internet sites and other informational material on the states of matter

• Informational material on the physics of sound waves

• Computer microphones

• A variety of instruments and other objects for producing sample sounds

Preparation

1. Review with students the general characteristics of waves, such as wavelength, frequency, amplitude, and speed.

2. Review with students the principles of concept mapping.

Lesson

1. Ask students to form teams of two or three and develop a concept map on the physics of sound. Encourage teams to reference informational material on the subject as needed.

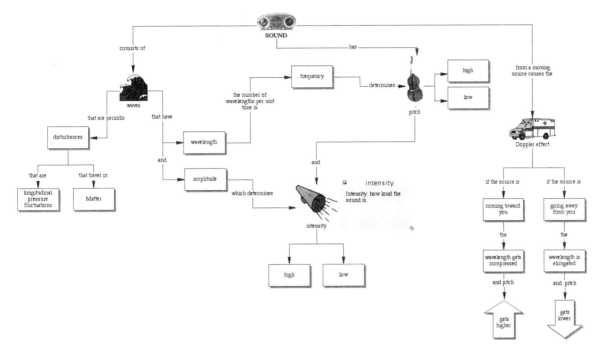

2. Have teams use the provided instruments and objects to create illustrative sounds for such concepts as pitch, intensity, and the Doppler effect. Instruct teams to add these sounds to their concept maps by selecting the appropriate symbols and choosing the Record command on the Tools menu.

3. Have teams present their concept maps to the class. Invite students to ask clarifying questions and offer suggestions. To play back audio samples, instruct each team to select the appropriate symbol and click on the Audio Quick Control.

4. Allow time for teams to revise their concept maps based on feedback.

Optometry Physics

Overview

In this lesson, students explore the characteristics of light by creating a presentation on the physics of sight.

Standard

Students examine the properties of light and optics.

Materials needed

• Internet sources and other informational material on the following subjects:

- Functional anatomy of the human eye

- Vision abnormalities such as astigmatism, nearsightedness, farsightedness, presbyopia, and color blindness

- Physics of light and color, effect of thin lenses on light, and examples of ray diagrams

- Strategies for correcting vision abnormalities

• Microsoft® PowerPoint®

Preparation

Make arrangements for students to present to various health or biology classes.

Lesson

1. Tell students they will deliver a PowerPoint® presentation on the physics of vision for a health or biology class at school. As a class, brainstorm a list of topics to include in the presentation and record them in an Inspiration® diagram using the RapidFire® tool. Save the diagram for student reference.

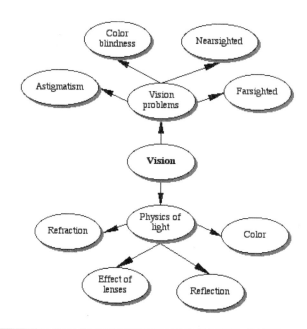

2. Ask students to form teams of four and encourage them to consult the provided informational material on the physics of light and its use in diagnosing and correcting vision problems.

3. Instruct teams to open Inspiration and switch to Outline View to record their research. Encourage them to use the Hyperlink tool to link appropriate symbols with web sites that feature such images as ray diagrams, color blindness tests, and the visual spectrum.

4. Circulate among the teams to monitor their progress and the accuracy of their information.

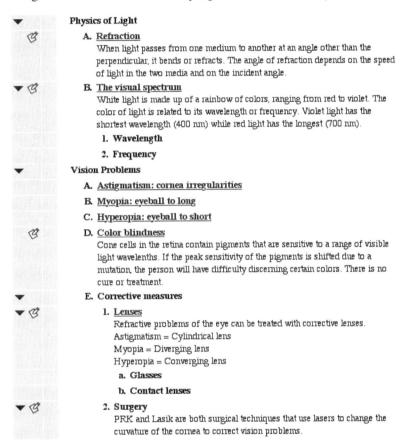

Physics of Light

   A. Refraction
      When light passes from one medium to another at an angle other than the perpendicular, it bends or refracts. The angle of refraction depends on the speed of light in the two media and on the incident angle.

   B. The visual spectrum
      White light is made up of a rainbow of colors, ranging from red to violet. The color of light is related to its wavelength or frequency. Violet light has the shortest wavelength (400 nm) while red light has the longest (700 nm).
      1. Wavelength
      2. Frequency

Vision Problems

   A. Astigmatism: cornea irregularities
   B. Myopia: eyeball to long
   C. Hyperopia: eyeball to short
   D. Color blindness
      Cone cells in the retina contain pigments that are sensitive to a range of visible light wavelenths. If the peak sensitivity of the pigments is shifted due to a mutation, the person will have difficulty discerning certain colors. There is no cure or treatment.
   E. Corrective measures
      1. Lenses
      Refractive problems of the eye can be treated with corrective lenses.
      Astigmatism = Cylindrical lens
      Myopia = Diverging lens
      Hyperopia = Converging lens
        a. Glasses
        b. Contact lenses
      2. Surgery
      PRK and Lasik are both surgical techniques that use lasers to change the curvature of the cornea to correct vision problems.

5. Ask teams to select Export on the File menu. In the dialog box, have them choose the PowerPoint export and click Save. Allow time for teams to finalize their work in PowerPoint. They can continue to use the Inspiration outline to reference images they located earlier on the Internet. Remind teams to cite sources when using print or Internet material.

6. Instruct teams to meet with another team and practice their presentations. Encourage students to offer constructive feedback. Allow time for teams to revise their diagrams.

7. Have teams deliver their presentations to health or biology classes in the school.

Introduction to the Periodic Table

Overview

Understanding the relationship between the electron configuration of an element and its chemical behavior and position on the periodic table is essential to the broader study of chemistry. In this lesson, students investigate this relationship by analyzing the first eighteen elements of the periodic table in an Inspiration® diagram.

Standard

Students know how the electron configuration of atoms governs the chemical properties of an element.

Materials needed

• Periodic tables available for reference

• Informational material on the electron configuration and chemistry of the first eighteen elements

Preparation

1. Download the following Electron Configuration template at www.inspiration.com/inscience or create your own version and save it using the Inspiration Template Wizard.

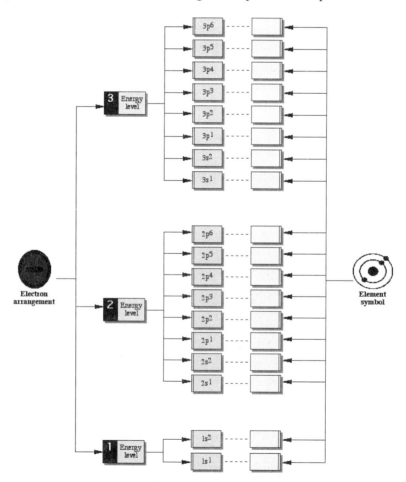

2. Review with students such concepts as atomic number, structure of the electron cloud, and ionic and covalent bonding.

Lesson

1. Ask students to consult the informational material on the electron arrangement of the first eighteen elements in the periodic table. Have them open the Electron Configuration template and enter each element's symbol into the appropriate template symbol.

2. Instruct students to research the chemical behavior of the first eighteen elements.

3. Using the information they have gathered up to this point, challenge students to meaningfully diagram the relationship of each element's electron configuration to the element's position on the periodic table and its subsequent chemical behavior.

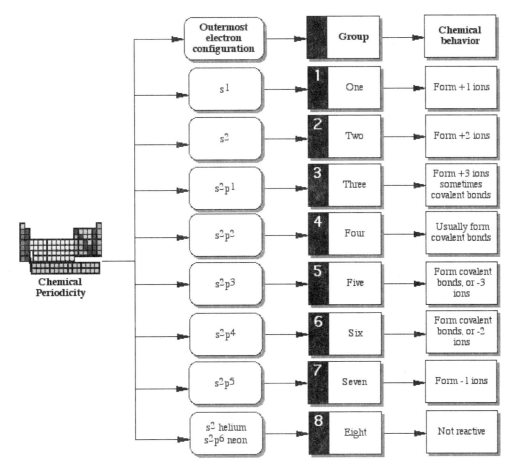

4. Ask students to speculate on the chemical behavior of other representative elements such as K, Ca, Br, and Kr. This discussion can serve as an introduction to a more detailed study of the periodic table.

Ionic Compound Formulas

Overview

Writing ionic compound formulas requires an understanding of the role of valence electrons in the formation of a chemical bond. In this lesson, students use Inspiration® to explore the principles of writing ionic compound formulas. This lesson can be used as a formative assessment tool for a unit on ionic bonding.

Standards

• Students know how atoms form bonds.
• Students know how the electron configuration of atoms governs the chemical properties of an element.

Preparation

1. Engage students in learning activities on such concepts as the octet rule, electron transfer, ionic bonding, and rules for writing ionic compound formulas.

2. Download the following Chemical Formula Rubric template at www.inspiration.com/inscience, or create your own version and save it using the Inspiration Template Wizard.

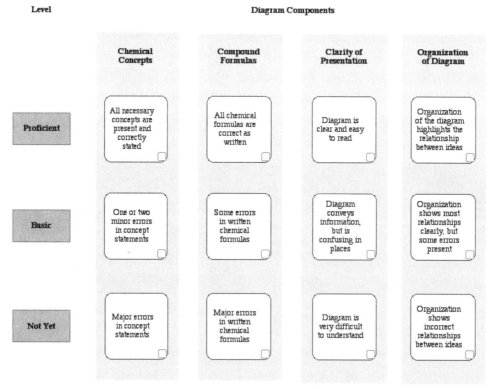

Level	Chemical Concepts	Compound Formulas	Clarity of Presentation	Organization of Diagram
Proficient	All necessary concepts are present and correctly stated	All chemical formulas are correct as written	Diagram is clear and easy to read	Organization of the diagram highlights the relationship between ideas
Basic	One or two minor errors in concept statements	Some errors in written chemical formulas	Diagram conveys information, but is confusing in places	Organization shows most relationships clearly, but some errors present
Not Yet	Major errors in concept statements	Major errors in written chemical formulas	Diagram is very difficult to understand	Organization shows incorrect relationships between ideas

Lesson

1. Have students form teams of two or three and instruct them to create an Inspiration diagram illustrating the principles and procedures of writing ionic compound formulas.

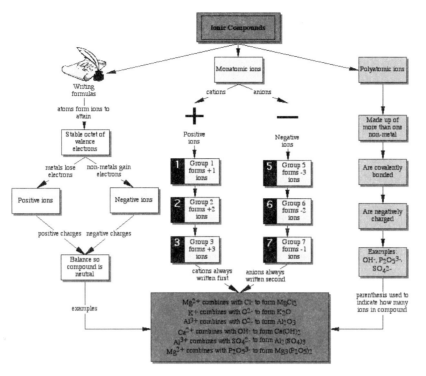

2. Ask teams to exchange copies of their diagrams with two other teams.

3. Instruct teams to evaluate the other teams' diagrams using the Chemical Formula Rubric template (one rubric per diagram). Have teams rate diagram components as Proficient, Basic, or Not Yet by checking off the appropriate symbol. Ask them to add a note to the checked symbols to record what problems exist, if any, and recommendations for correction.

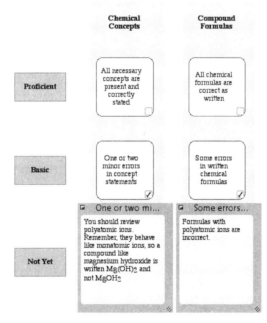

4. Have teams print two copies of each rubric and distribute one to you and one to the team whose diagram they evaluated. Remind them before printing to confirm that notes are open and all notes text is visible.

5. Ask students to revise their diagrams based on other teams' feedback.

Stoichiometry

Overview

How many grams of product yield a given amount of reactant? What amount of reactant determines the yield of a chemical reaction? These are fundamental questions in chemistry. In order to answer them, students need to know the basic quantitative nature of chemical reactions. In this lesson, students complete a series of activities to build and assess their knowledge of the principles of stoichiometry.

Standard

Students know how to calculate the masses of reactants and products in a chemical reaction from the mass of one of the reactants or products, and the relevant atomic masses.

Preparation

1. Download the following Conversion Factors template at www.inspiration.com/inscience or create your own version and save it using the Inspiration® Template Wizard.

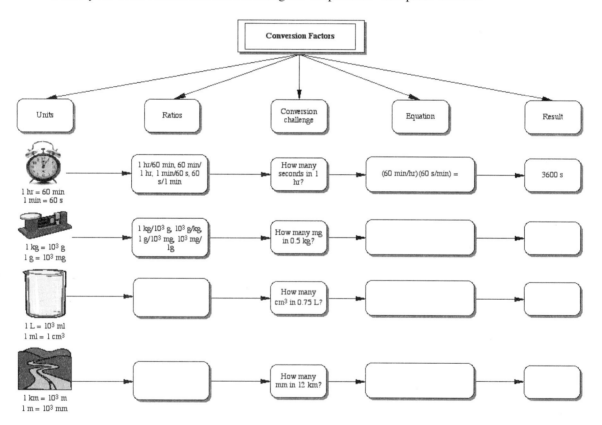

2. Prepare introductory learning activities on the topics of chemical quantities and stoichiometry.

3. Review with students how to write chemical formulas and balance chemical equations.

Lesson

CONVERSION FACTORS

1. Ask students to form teams of two and open the Conversion Factors template.

2. Instruct teams to complete operations described in the template and add at least three additional conversions to the diagram.

3. Have three or four teams get together and compare their completed diagrams. Ask them to develop a general procedure for using conversion factors to solve problems. Circulate among the teams, checking for accuracy and correcting any misconceptions.

NUMBERS AND MASS

4. Engage the class in a discussion of quantities that are made up of a specific number of units, for instance, a dozen, a case, and a gross. Ask them what the relationship is between the mass of an individual unit and the total mass of the quantity.

5. Ask students to form teams of three or four and create a diagram to calculate the mass of a quantity based on the mass of its individual components.

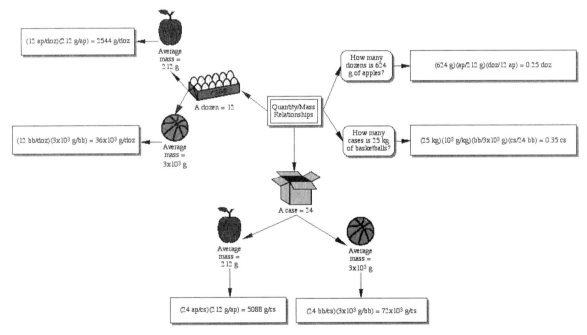

MOLES AND MASS

6. Lead students in an introductory learning activity on chemical quantities, covering such concepts as the mole, gram atomic mass, and molar mass.

Continued next page

continued

7. Engage students in a class discussion on the similarities between the mole and more common quantities, such as a dozen or a case.

8. Ask students to reform into their original teams and use the Thinking Skills—Idea Map template to record their understanding of moles, adding symbols and notes as needed.

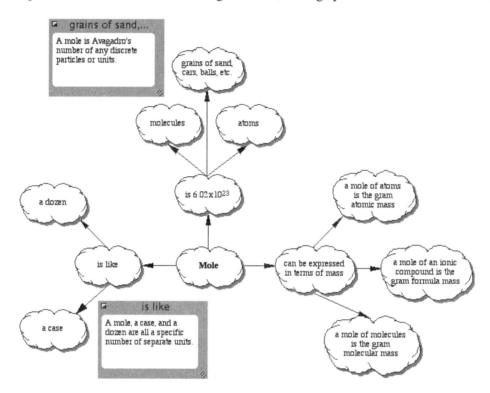

STOICHIOMETRY

9. Lead students in an introductory learning activity on stoichiometry.

10. Ask students to form teams of two or three, and challenge each team to construct a meaningful diagram that maps the necessary steps in the three major stoichiometric calculations: amount of product formed from a given amount of reactant, amount of reactant needed to produce a given amount of product, and determination of the limiting reagent.

Model equation: $2Fe_{(s)} + 3S_{(s)} = Fe_2S_3$

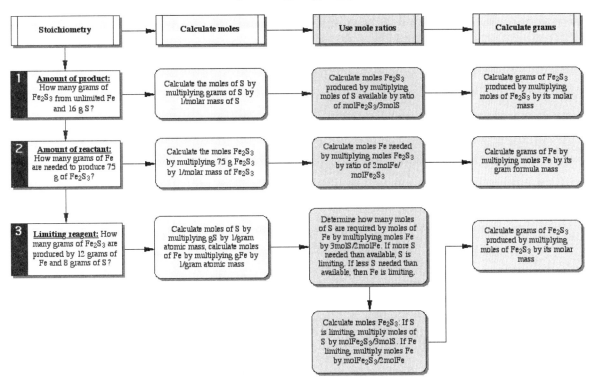

Stoichiometry	Calculate moles	Use mole ratios	Calculate grams
1 Amount of product: How many grams of Fe_2S_3 from unlimited Fe and 16 g S?	Calculate the moles of S by multiplying grams of S by 1/molar mass of S	Calculate moles Fe_2S_3 produced by multiplying moles of S available by ratio of molFe_2S_3/3molS	Calculate grams of Fe_2S_3 produced by multiplying moles of Fe_2S_3 by its molar mass
2 Amount of reactant: How many grams of Fe are needed to produce 75 g of Fe_2S_3?	Calculate the moles Fe_2S_3 by multiplying 75 g Fe_2S_3 by 1/molar mass of Fe_2S_3	Calculate moles Fe needed by multiplying moles Fe_2S_3 by ratio of 2molFe/ molFe_2S_3	Calculate grams of Fe by multiplying moles Fe by its gram formula mass
3 Limiting reagent: How many grams of Fe_2S_3 are produced by 12 grams of Fe and 8 grams of S?	Calculate moles of S by multiplying gS by 1/gram atomic mass, calculate moles of Fe by multiplying gFe by 1/gram atomic mass	Determine how many moles of S are required by moles of Fe by multiplying moles Fe by 3molS/2molFe. If more S needed than available, S is limiting. If less S needed than available, then Fe is limiting.	Calculate grams of Fe_2S_3 produced by multiplying moles of Fe_2S_3 by its molar mass

Calculate moles Fe_2S_3: If S is limiting, multiply moles of S by molFe_2S_3/3molS. If Fe limiting, multiply moles Fe by molFe_2S_3/2molFe

11. Encourage teams to share and discuss their diagrams with another team.

12. Suggest teams revise their diagrams based on feedback.

Acid-base Titration

Overview

In this lesson, students build their understanding of acid-base interactions and solution chemistry by designing an experiment to determine the molarity of an unknown acid by titration. This activity is useful as a summative performance assessment at the end of a unit on solutions.

Standards

- Students know acids are hydrogen ion donating substances and bases are hydrogen ion accepting substances.

- Students know how to calculate the concentration of a solute in terms of molarity.

- Students design and conduct scientific investigations.

Materials needed

- Burets
- Buret clamp
- Ring stand
- 125 ml Erlenmeyer flasks
- 1M HCL solution
- 1M NaOH solution
- Unknown monoprotic acid solution
- Phenophthalein indicator solution
- Distilled water

Preparation

1. Review with students solution chemistry, acid-base interactions, and laboratory safety procedures.

2. Review with students the principles of experimental design.

Lesson

1. Ask students to form teams of two and tell them their task is to determine the molarity of an unknown acid solution using the provided lab equipment.

2. Have teams use the Inspiration® Science—Experimental Design template to plan their experiment.

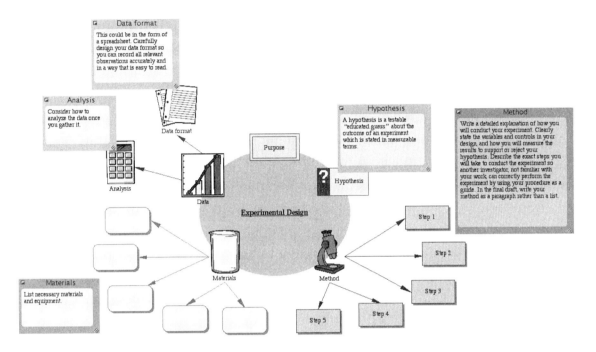

3. Instruct teams to enter design information into the appropriate symbols, adding details with the Note tool as needed. Remind teams that this procedure does not require a hypothesis.

4. Circulate among the teams as they work on their designs and check for thoroughness and understanding.

5. Ask four teams to group together and discuss their completed designs. Have teams revise their designs based on feedback.

6. Instruct teams to discuss their designs with you prior to checking out the necessary equipment for the experiment.

7. As teams conduct their experiments, monitor their progress and make sure they follow proper laboratory procedure.

Continued next page

8. Once the experiments are completed and the teams have analyzed their data, instruct them to open their Experimental Design diagram and switch to Outline View. Ask teams to add results and a conclusion to their outlines.

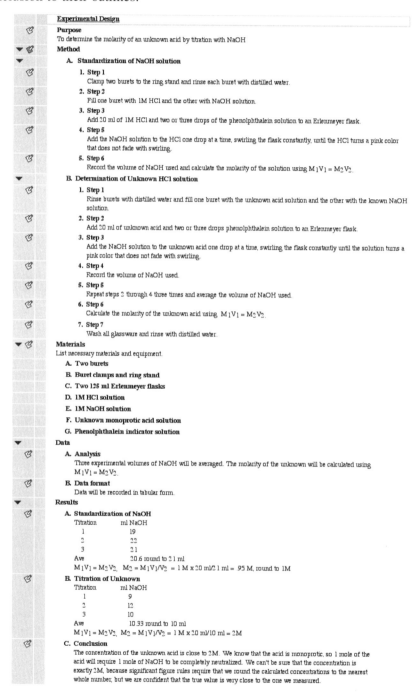

Experimental Design

Purpose
To determine the molarity of an unknown acid by titration with NaOH

Method

  A. Standardization of NaOH solution
   1. Step 1
      Clamp two burets to the ring stand and rinse each buret with distilled water.
   2. Step 2
      Fill one buret with 1M HCl and the other with NaOH solution.
   3. Step 3
      Add 20 ml of 1M HCl and two or three drops of the phenolphthalein solution to an Erlenmeyer flask.
   4. Step 5
      Add the NaOH solution to the HCl one drop at a time, swirling the flask constantly, until the HCl turns a pink color that does not fade with swirling.
   5. Step 6
      Record the volume of NaOH used and calculate the molarity of the solution using $M_1V_1 = M_2V_2$.

  B. Determination of Unknown HCl solution
   1. Step 1
      Rinse burets with distilled water and fill one buret with the unknown acid solution and the other with the known NaOH solution.
   2. Step 2
      Add 20 ml of unknown acid and two or three drops phenolphthalein solution to an Erlenmeyer flask.
   3. Step 3
      Add the NaOH solution to the unknown acid one drop at a time, swirling the flask constantly until the solution turns a pink color that does not fade with swirling.
   4. Step 4
      Record the volume of NaOH used.
   5. Step 5
      Repeat steps 2 through 4 three times and average the volume of NaOH used.
   6. Step 6
      Calculate the molarity of the unknown acid using $M_1V_1 = M_2V_2$.
   7. Step 7
      Wash all glassware and rinse with distilled water.

Materials
List necessary materials and equipment.
  A. Two burets
  B. Buret clamps and ring stand
  C. Two 125 ml Erlenmeyer flasks
  D. 1M HCl solution
  E. 1M NaOH solution
  F. Unknown monoprotic acid solution
  G. Phenolphthalein indicator solution

Data

  A. Analysis
    Three experimental volumes of NaOH will be averaged. The molarity of the unknown will be calculated using $M_1V_1 = M_2V_2$.

  B. Data format
    Data will be recorded in tabular form.

Results

  A. Standardization of NaOH

Titration	ml NaOH
1	19
2	22
3	21
Ave	20.6 round to 21 ml

$M_1V_1 = M_2V_2$, $M_2 = M_1V_1/V_2 = 1\,M \times 20\ ml/21\ ml = .95\,M$, round to 1M

  B. Titration of Unknown

Titration	ml NaOH
1	9
2	12
3	10
Ave	10.33 round to 10 ml

$M_1V_1 = M_2V_2$, $M_2 = M_1V_1/V_2 = 1\,M \times 20\ ml/10\ ml = 2M$

  C. Conclusion
    The concentration of the unknown acid is close to 2M. We know that the acid is monoprotic, so 1 mole of the acid will require 1 mole of NaOH to be completely neutralized. We can't be sure that the concentration is exactly 2M, because significant figure rules require that we round the calculated concentrations to the nearest whole number, but we are confident that the true value is very close to the one we measured.

9. Have students click the Transfer button to finalize their formal lab report in a word processor.

Earth Science

Climate Comparison

Overview

Atmospheric and geographical characteristics such as air pressure, rainfall, large bodies of water, and mountain ranges influence the climate of any given region. In this lesson, students use weather data to compare and contrast the climates of two locations and relate the observed differences to the local and regional geography.

Standard

Students know various factors that affect weather patterns.

Materials needed

- The National Oceanic and Atmospheric Administration's Climate Diagnostics Center web site, www.cdc.noaa.gov/USclimate/states.fast.html
- Informational material on the effects of geographical features on climate
- Several United States atlases

Preparation

Familiarize yourself with the NOAA web site.

Lesson

1. Ask students to form teams of two to four and instruct them to select two cities in the United States to research. Encourage them to select locations that are geographically different.

2. For each location, have teams research the region's climate using the NOAA web site. Instruct them to gather data covering one month within each season, and focus on parameters such as precipitation, maximum and minimum temperatures, and daily sunlight totals.

3. Ask students to open the Inspiration® Thinking Skills—Comparison template and record their observations in the appropriate symbols.

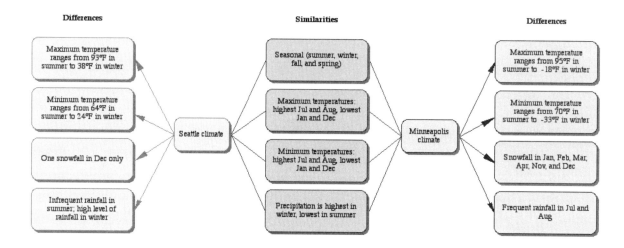

Differences

- Maximum temperature ranges from 93°F in summer to 38°F in winter
- Minimum temperature ranges from 64°F in summer to 24°F in winter
- One snowfall in Dec only
- Infrequent rainfall in summer; high level of rainfall in winter

Seattle climate

Similarities

- Seasonal (summer, winter, fall, and spring)
- Maximum temperatures: highest Jul and Aug, lowest Jan and Dec
- Minimum temperatures: highest Jul and Aug, lowest Jan and Dec
- Precipitation is highest in winter, lowest in summer

Minneapolis climate

Differences

- Maximum temperature ranges from 95°F in summer to -18°F in winter
- Minimum temperature ranges from 70°F in summer to -33°F in winter
- Snowfall in Jan, Feb, Mar, Apr, Nov, and Dec
- Frequent rainfall in Jul and Aug

4. Have teams consult a United States atlas to research the physical geography of their chosen cities. Tell them to pay particular attention to the proximity of oceans, mountain ranges, and large lakes.

5. Encourage students to consult the informational material on the influence of geographical features on climate.

6. Ask teams to create a new diagram comparing the geography and climate of the cities they researched. Have them use the Hyperlink tool to connect the climate data on the NOAA web site to the appropriate symbols.

7. Have teams present their diagrams to the class, clicking on the hyperlinked text to display supporting data. Encourage the class to look for common patterns.

8. Based on the information presented, engage the class in a discussion on how geography influences climate.

9. Give students geographical information about a city that has not been researched and ask them to speculate on its climate. Provide them with the city's climatological data and invite them to assess the accuracy of their predictions.

The Reason for Seasons

Overview

In this lesson, students explore why the Earth's climate is seasonal and increase their understanding of planetary motion, the importance of solar radiation, and the effect of physical processes on the distribution and abundance of living things.

Standard

Students know how the tilt of the Earth's axis and the Earth's revolution around the Sun affect seasons and day length.

Materials needed

- Informational material on the climate of selected locations in the Northern and Southern Hemispheres

- One setup per team:

    - Desktop world globe

    - Light source, such as a lamp without a shade

    - Measuring tape

    - String

Preparation

Familiarize yourself with the NOAA web site.

Lesson

1. Have students brainstorm possible causes of seasonal change. Record their ideas in an Inspiration® diagram using the RapidFire® tool and save it for student reference.

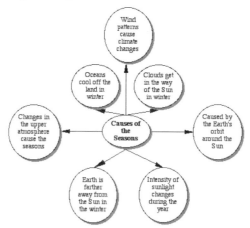

2. Ask students to form teams of three or four. Have them consult the provided informational material to research monthly maximum and minimum temperature data for five locations in both the Northern and Southern Hemispheres.

3. Instruct teams to present their findings to the class.

4. Revisit the brainstorm diagram with the class. Encourage students to reevaluate their original ideas on seasonal change in light of their research. Have them decide which ideas are still reasonable explanations.

5. Distribute globes and other materials to each team. Ask them to construct a circle with a diameter of 1.5 m on the floor. Have them use string to mark off the perimeter of the circle.

6. Tell teams to model the Sun by placing the light source at the center of the circle on a desk.

7. Have a member of each team simulate the orbit of the Earth around the Sun by holding the globe and walking around the perimeter of the circle. Instruct them to make sure the axis of the Earth always points to the same location in the room.

8. Ask students to observe and record which hemisphere of the Earth is tilted toward or away from the Sun at different positions in the orbit, and which positions result in the most direct and intense sunlight for each hemisphere.

9. Lead a discussion with the class on the seasonal effect of the Earth's tilt as it orbits the Sun. Reference the brainstorm diagram to note student misconceptions not yet addressed.

10. Instruct teams to use all the information gathered to construct a concept map illustrating the causes of the seasons.

Extension

- Ask each team to do a presentation on seasonal change for an elementary school class. In preparation, instruct teams to print their concept maps over six to nine pages to create a poster. To do so, use the Scale Diagram option found in the Page Setup dialog. Provide tape and scissors to teams to construct their posters.

- For the presentations, encourage each team to use models to demonstrate Earth's orbit and its relationship to seasonal change. Have them discuss their concept map and leave it with the elementary class for student reference.

Exploring the Solar System

Overview

In this lesson, students research planets and create a Solar System web site for use by early elementary students.

Standard

Students know the characteristics and movement patterns of objects in the Solar System.

Materials needed

• Informational material on our Solar System, such as The National Air and Space Museum's web site, www.nasm.si.edu/ceps/etp

• Examples of nonfiction reading material developed for early elementary students

Preparation

1. Download the following Planet template at www.inspiration.com/inscience or create your own version and save it using the Inspiration® Template Wizard.

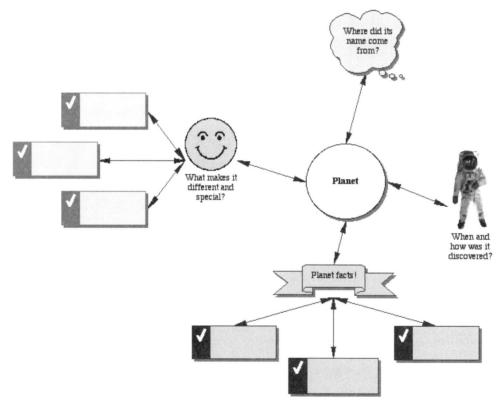

2. You may find it useful to download the Solar System example at www.inspiration.com/inscience.

3. Contact a local elementary school and make arrangements for your class to visit and present their web site project to young students.

Lesson

1. Divide the class into ten teams and assign a planet or the asteroid belt to each team.

2. Instruct the teams to research their planet using the provided informational material. Have each team open the Planet template and enter their findings into the appropriate symbols. Encourage them to use the Create tool and the Note tool to record further details.

3. Ask teams to consult the early elementary reading materials. Instruct them to revise and reorganize their diagram so it is appropriate for young students' understanding and reading level. Inform them that each symbol and its associated note will be a separate page on the web site. Remind them to use double-headed arrows for each link.

Continued next page

4. As teams work on their designs, circulate and check for understanding and thoroughness.

5. Have teams discuss their designs with you prior to checking out the equipment and materials necessary for the experiment.

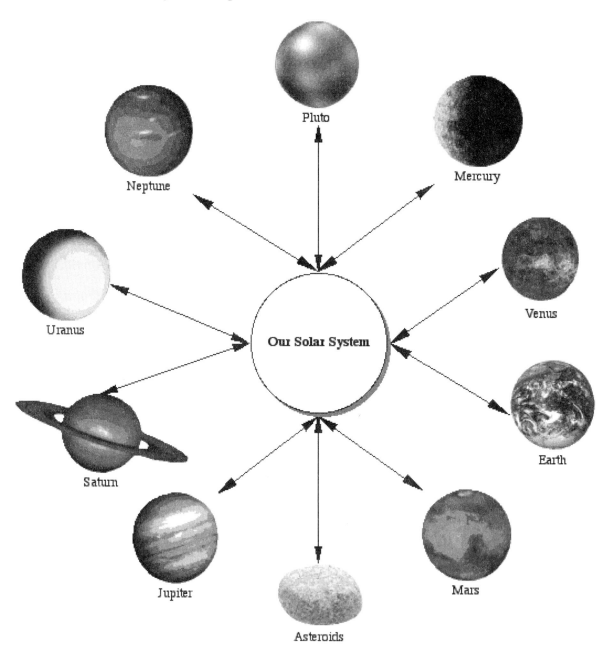

6. Use the Hyperlink tool to connect each team's diagram to the appropriate symbol.

7. Export the Solar System diagram using the Export as HTML option on the File menu. Select the Site Skeleton® export to create the foundation of the web site.

8. Have teams use web site authoring software to finalize their portion of the web site.

9. Ask students to prepare for the visit to a local elementary classroom. Have teams work together to create a brief list of grade level appropriate questions that elementary students could answer by exploring the Solar System web site. Compile the questions in Inspiration's Outline View to form a simple worksheet. Print the worksheets and make copies for distribution to the elementary students.

10. During the visit, have students present the web site and hand out the worksheets, then observe and assist the elementary students as they navigate the web site and research answers. Later, teams may wish to modify their portion of the web site based on their observations.

Tectonics

Overview

The study of plate tectonics answers such questions as why volcanoes ring the Pacific Ocean, what causes earthquakes, and how and why mountain ranges are formed. In this lesson, students research plate tectonics and present the information in a concept map.

Standard

Students understand the concept of plate tectonics and the evidence that supports it.

Materials needed

Informational material on plate tectonics, such as the United States Geological Survey's online edition of "This Dynamic Earth," http://pubs.usgs.gov/publications/text/dynamic.html

Preparation

1. Discuss with students these and other characteristics of the Earth's surface that were difficult to explain prior to the development of plate tectonic theory:

- The Pacific Ocean is ringed with active volcanoes.
- The floor of the Pacific Ocean has deep trenches close to active volcanoes.
- The ocean floor has an extensive ridge system with hydrothermal vents.
- Ocean floor sediments are much thinner than they should be if the oceans are billions of years old.

2. Invite students to brainstorm possible explanations for these facts.

3. Review principles of concept mapping with students.

Lesson

1. Ask students to form teams of three and have each team member choose one of the following aspects of plate tectonics to investigate: early theory, supporting evidence, and effects.

2. Instruct each team's members to research their chosen topic using the provided informational material and use Inspiration® to illustrate their findings in a concept map.

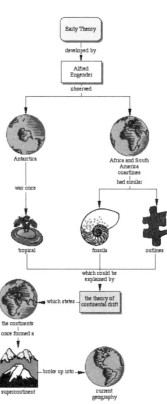

3. Ask teams to open a new Inspiration diagram and copy and paste their individual concept maps into the new diagram. Have them create a plate tectonics concept map by using the Link tool to connect each team member's contribution. Encourage them to modify the diagram for clarity.

4. Have teams present their completed concept maps to the class. Encourage students to ask clarifying questions and offer suggestions for improvement.

5. Allow time for teams to revise their concepts maps based on feedback.

The Life of a Star

Overview

Stars are dynamic and evolving objects in which the inward pull of gravity is counterbalanced by the energy produced by nuclear fusion. In this lesson, students research the life cycle of stars and convey the information in a concept map.

Standard

Students know the ongoing processes involved in star formation and destruction.

Materials needed

NASA web site, "Imagine the Universe," http://imagine.gsfc.nasa.gov

Preparation

1. Review with students the physics of nuclear fusion and gravity.

2. Review with students the principles of concept mapping.

Lesson

1. Ask students to form teams of two or three, and have them brainstorm everything they know about stars and their life cycles. Instruct them to record this information in an Inspiration® diagram using the RapidFire® tool. Have them save the diagrams for reference.

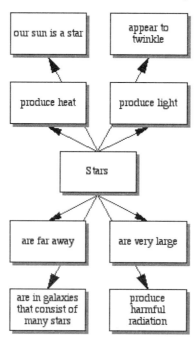

2. Encourage teams to visit the NASA "Imagine the Universe" web site to research the life cycles of stars.

3. Instruct each team to use the information they gather to create a concept map.

4. Have teams present their concept maps to the class. Invite students to ask clarifying questions and offer suggestions.

5. Allow time for teams to revise their concept maps based on feedback.

6. Have students refer to their concept maps and earlier brainstorm diagrams as they write a paragraph about what they learned and how their understanding of the star cycle may have changed. In particular, ask them to reflect on the role of gravity in the life and death of stars.

Water Conservation Project

Overview

The amount of fresh water available in a given locality is a function of natural processes, such as the water cycle, and patterns of human usage. In this lesson, students use Inspiration® to design and implement a water conservation education project for the community.

Standard

Students understand the factors that influence water quality, supply, use, reuse, recycling, conservation, and management.

Preparation

1. Download the following templates at www.inspiration.com/inscience or create your own versions and save them using the Inspiration Template Wizard.

PROJECT PLANNING TEMPLATE

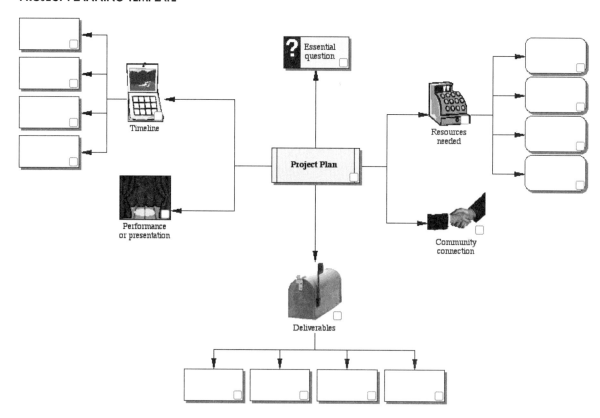

PROJECT PROGRESS TEMPLATE

PRESENTATION DESIGN TEMPLATE

2. From the "Project-based Instruction Templates" on page 98, use the Project Design and Project Management templates to develop the underlying scaffold for the project.

3. Contact community organizations that would be good project resources (for example, public works department, state and federal fish and wildlife departments, city and county parks departments, soil and water conservation districts, and watershed councils). Identify experts from various fields who are willing to present information and work with your students.

Continued next page

→ **Lesson**

PREPARATION

1. Inform students their task is to design a program to educate the community about a local water conservation issue.

2. Invite experts from one or more of the agencies you contacted to make a presentation to the class on local water conservation issues. Have students note the problems identified by the speaker.

3. As a class, discuss which of the problems would be most suitable for a community education project.

4. Divide the class into teams of four and have each team select an aspect of the issue to research. For example, if the issue is the desire to restore a remnant of flood plain habitat located in a city park, teams might research the following topics: the history of flood plain loss on the river, the importance of flood plains to the river, possible techniques of restoration, suitable plant species and where to find them, and animals that depend on flood plain habitats.

5. Have each team open the Project Planning template in Inspiration and plan their portion of the project by recording information in the appropriate symbols. Encourage students to use the Note tool to add notes and record additional details.

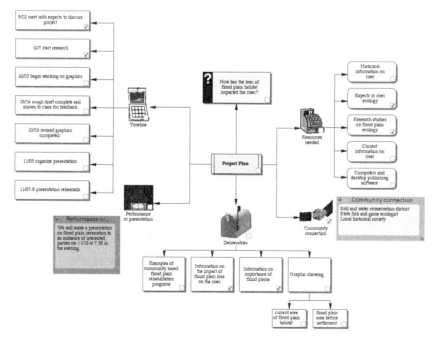

6. Have each team present their plan to the class. Invite students to ask questions and offer suggestions.

7. Engage the class in a discussion on ways to effectively present the results of the water conservation project.

8. As a class, assign team responsibilities for the presentation. Instruct teams to record their tasks in the subtopics of the symbol labeled "Deliverables" in their planning diagram.

RESEARCH AND IMPLEMENTATION

9. As teams research their project assignments, suggest they use the Planning—Research Strategy template to record their findings.

10. Remind teams that planning, researching, and implementing a project is not a linear process. Teams will likely need to revisit and modify their plans throughout their investigations because of new information and unforeseen complications.

11. At regular intervals during the research and implementation phase, conduct formative assessments to monitor each team's progress. Instruct teams to use the Project Progress template to record developments and issues as they arise, then provide these to you for review and discussion.

PRESENTATION

12. As a class, design the chosen performance or exhibition using the Presentation Design template. Take into account changes that were made to the project during the course of team investigations.

Continued next page

13. Instruct students to write and distribute letters of invitation to the selected audience.

14. After the performance or exhibition, review with students the audience feedback gathered using the feedback strategies identified in the Presentation Design diagram.

15. Have students write a reflective essay covering the following topics:

- What did they learn about water conservation?
- How well did their team work together?
- How did they overcome difficulties encountered during the project?
- How did community members contribute to the project?
- How would they change their project based on the feedback they received after the presentation?

Teaching Resources

Concept Mapping with Inspiration®

Overview

Concept maps encourage understanding by helping students organize and enhance their knowledge on any topic. They help students learn new information by integrating each new idea into their existing body of knowledge.

Concept maps are ideal for measuring the growth of student learning. As students create concept maps, they restate ideas using their own words. Misdirected links or wrong connections alert educators to what students do not understand, providing an accurate, objective way to evaluate areas in which students do not yet grasp concepts fully.

Preparation

Discuss with students the purpose and attributes of a concept map. Show several examples of varying complexity.

Lesson

1. Provide to students, or ask them to identify, a single concept upon which to base a concept map. For example, in the study of biology, students might start with the concept of bacteria.

2. Ask students to open a new Inspiration® diagram and enter the concept into the Main Idea symbol.

3. Instruct students to use point and type to create symbols for all the major terms or topics associated with the initial concept.

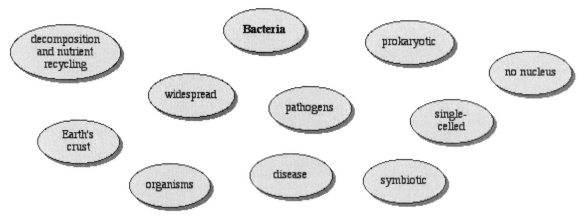

4. Have students use the Link tool to link related symbols. In each link's associated text box, enter words that explain the relationship between the ideas. To aid student thinking, remind them that in a concept map it is possible to read symbols and their connecting link text as sentences. Encourage students to add additional concepts as needed.

5. Encourage students to use the Note tool to add notes and record explanatory information.

6. Ask students to rearrange and modify symbols and links so relationships are clear and the completed map is easily understood. Point out to students that many concepts maps are organized so general topics are at the top, flowing down to more specific subtopics at the bottom.

The Concept Map template

The Inspiration Science—Concept Map template offers students another way to develop a concept map. Some students may find it helpful to see the general structure of a concept map and start with a few symbols and links already created.

Student-designed Investigation Templates

Overview

National and state science standards stress the importance of student participation in the design and implementation of scientific investigations. Students are asked to identify a question to study, design a research strategy, analyze the results, and communicate their conclusions. These templates help develop and assess student-designed investigations.

Student Investigation Planning template

Download the following Student Investigation Planning template at www.inspiration.com/inscience, or create your own version and save it using the Inspiration® Template Wizard.

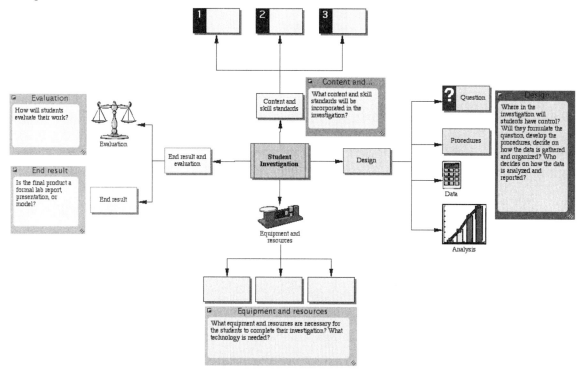

There is no prescribed order for planning investigations, but the completed design should address all the elements found in the template.

Assessment and Evaluation template

Download the following Assessment and Evaluation template at www.inspiration.com/inscience, or create your own version and save it using the Inspiration Template Wizard.

Use this template to develop formative assessments and create a final evaluation for student-conducted scientific investigations.

Project-based Instruction Templates

Overview

Project-based learning is a powerful methodology that can provide rigorous, relevant learning experiences for meeting state and national standards. Students working on projects not only master academic content and skills, they apply them in a variety of contexts outside the classroom. The following templates aid the design and management of project-based learning activities.

Project Design Template

Download the following Project Design template at www.inspiration.com/inscience or create your own version and save it using the Inspiration® Template Wizard.

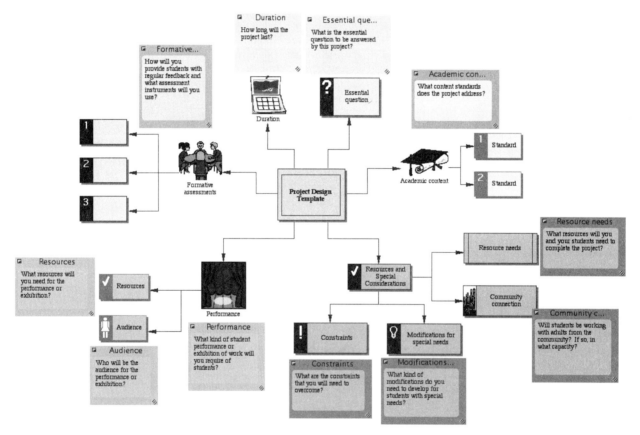

There is no prescribed order for planning a project, but the completed design should address all the elements found in the template.

Project Management Template

Download the following Project Management template at www.inspiration.com/inscience or create your own version and save it using the Inspiration Template Wizard.

Use this template to plan the sequence and timing of project activities by entering information into the appropriate symbols. Use the Create tool and the Note tool to record additional details.

Performance Task Templates

Overview

Performance tasks are rich, multi-faceted learning activities that require students to master concepts and information, apply what they have learned, develop skills, and communicate the results of their efforts. Because of the complexity of performance tasks, they can be challenging to design. The following templates assist in the development of powerful and engaging performance tasks for students.

Performance Task Design template

Download the following Performance Task Design template at www.inspiration.com/inscience or create your own version and save it using the Inspiration® Template Wizard.

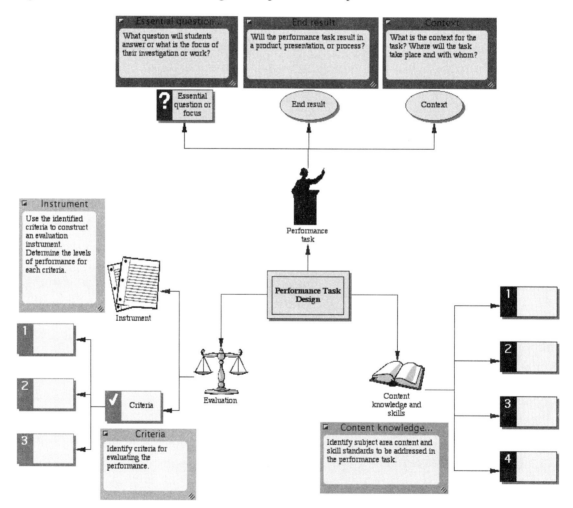

There is no prescribed order for planning performance tasks, but the completed design should address all the elements found in the template.

Performance Task Scaffold template

Download the following Performance Task Scaffold template at www.inspiration.com/inscience or create your own version and save it using the Inspiration Template Wizard.

Use this template to design the supporting scaffold for the performance task and ensure student readiness for its successful completion.

How To

This section provides a step-by-step guide for using Inspiration® features, such as the Template Wizard and Site Skeleton™, that are especially helpful in lesson preparation, design, and implementation.

How to Create Templates

Overview

Educators often create their own templates to use as a starting point for a special project or assignment. The Inspiration® Template Wizard walks you step-by-step through saving any Inspiration document as a template.

To create a template:

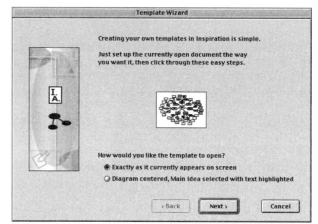

1. Create the diagram or outline you want to save as a template.

2. On the Utility menu, choose Template Wizard.

3. Choose how you want the template to open, and then click Next.

4. Choose the symbol defaults for the template, and then click Next.

The document's current default settings are displayed. To use the Inspiration program's default settings, click Factory Settings.

5. Choose the link defaults for the template, and then click Next.

6. Choose the note defaults for the template, and then click Next.

7. Choose the outline defaults for the template, and then click Next.

8. Choose printing defaults for Diagram View and Outline View, and then click Next.

9. In the Save dialog box, choose the folder where you want to save the template. Inspiration automatically opens the Inspiration Templates folder, but you can choose any folder.

10. In the Name box, type a name for the template.

11. Click Save. In Windows the file is saved with an IST extension.

12. To set the newly created template as the default template for the Inspiration program, select the Set as Default check box in the Success dialog box. When you choose this option, all new Inspiration documents will be based on the newly created template.

How to Create New Symbol Libraries

Overview

Inspiration® makes it easy to create custom libraries for imported graphics and images created using the draw tools. Educators can copy frequently used symbols into a custom library, and create custom libraries for special projects or class assignments.

To create a symbol library:

1. On the Utility menu, choose New Symbol Library.

The Add New Library dialog box appears.

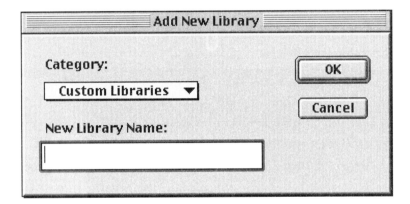

2. On the Category menu, choose the category you want the new library to appear under.

Note: You can place a symbol library under any category on the Symbol palette. If you do not choose a category, Inspiration places a new symbol library under the Custom category.

3. In the New Library Name box, type a name for the library.

4. Click OK to create the library or click Cancel to exit without creating a new library.

How to Transfer Work to a Word Processor

Overview

Students and educators can easily move an Inspiration® project to a word processor to format and edit the project for publication. The new document retains the look and structure of the Inspiration outline. When transferring from Diagram View, a picture of the diagram also appears.

Here are some things to consider about the Transfer tool, especially when creating templates that will serve as the basis for a word-processed composition:

• The prefix style selected in Outline View appears in the word processing document whether transferring from Outline View or Diagram View. To transfer without prefixes to a word processing document, select the No Prefix option using the Prefix tool on the Formatting toolbar in Outline View.

• The margins set in the Inspiration project transfer to the word processing document.

To transfer work to a word processor:

1. Open the Inspiration diagram or outline you want to transfer.

2. On the Toolbar, click the Transfer button.

3. On the File menu, choose Transfer to Word Processor.

4. Inspiration creates a new .doc or .rtf file in the same location as the Inspiration document and starts your preferred word processor.

How to Use the Site Skeleton® Export

Overview

The Site Skeleton® export allows educators to transform a diagram into the foundation of a web site, including a clickable site map. The Site Skeleton export makes each symbol or topic a separate page in the web site. All notes text appears on the page corresponding to the symbol or topic to which it was associated. Links in the diagram become hyperlinks on the web pages. Arrows show hyperlink direction.

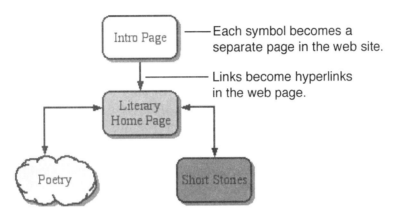

To use the Site Skeleton export:

1. On the File menu, choose Export as HTML. The Export to HTML dialog box appears.

2. Under Start Pages, choose Site Skeleton.

3. Click Save. The Save As dialog box appears.

4. Navigate to the folder where you want to save the HTML file.

5. Enter a name for the HTML file. Inspiration® automatically uses your main idea as the name and assigns the appropriate file extension, but you can change it if you want.

6. Click Save. The project is saved as a set of HTML files which can be finished using an HTML authoring tool.

Note: When creating a web site, you may wish to use links with two-headed arrows. This signifies that there are hyperlinks back and forth between two pages, while single-headed arrows make a hyperlink in one direction only. To create a two-headed arrow, on the Link menu, choose Arrow Direction, and then select Both Arrows.

Suggested Reading

Anders, G. & Beech, L.W. (1990). *Reading: Mapping for meaning: 70 graphic organizers for comprehension.* Kent, CT: Sniffen Court Books.

Ausubel, D. (1968). *Educational psychology: A cognitive view.* New York: Holt, Reinhart and Winston.

Bellanca, J. (1990). *The cooperative think tank: Graphic organizers to teach thinking in the cooperative classroom.* Arlington Heights, IL: IRI/SkyLight Training and Publishing, Inc.

Drapeau, P. (1998). *Great teaching with graphic organizers: Lessons and fun-shaped templates that motivate kids of all learning styles.* New York: Scholastic Professional Books.

Llewellyn, D. (2002). *Inquire within: Implementing inquiry-based science standards.* Thousand Oaks, CA: Corwin Press, Inc.

Marzano, R.J., Pickering, D.J. & Pollack, J.E. (2001). *Classroom instruction that works: Research-based strategies for increasing student achievement.* Alexandria, VA: Association for Supervision and Curriculum Development.

Novak, J.D. (1998). *Learning, creating and using knowledge: Concept maps™ as facilitative tools in schools and corporations.* Mahwah, NJ: Lawrence Erlbaum Associates, Inc.

Novak, J.D. & Gowin, D.B. (1984). *Learning how to learn.* New York: Cambridge University Press.

Roblyer, M.D. & Edwards, J. (2000). *Integrating educational technology into teaching.* Upper Saddle River, NJ: Prentice-Hall, Inc.

Rogers, S. & Graham, S. (2000). *The high performance toolbox: Succeeding with performance tasks, projects, and assessments.* Evergreen, CO: Peak Learning Systems, Inc.

Tarquin, P. & Walker, S. (1997). *Creating success in the classroom: Visual organizers and how to use them.* Englewood, CO: Teacher Ideas Press.

Thornburg, D.D. (1998). *Brainstorms and lightening bolts: Thinking skills for the 21st century.* San Carlos, CA: Starsong Publications.

About the Author

Bob Madar

Bob Madar is a Curriculum Designer for Inspiration Software®, Inc. with 14 years experience teaching science at the high school level. In 1997, he received a McAuliffe award for excellence in science teaching and, in 1999, his field studies course was featured in "Learning that Works" produced by WGBH Television. Mr. Madar has also provided training in inquiry-based science instruction, project-based learning, and small learning community development to schools and school districts throughout the United States.

Lesson Plan Books

Successfully integrate visual learning into your classroom

Discover a wealth of ideas to engage learners and improve performance with activities that encourage students to learn, think and create. Educators new to using Kidspiration® and Inspiration® get started integrating visual learning more quickly and effectively, veteran users are inspired with new ideas and trainers are able to customize workshops with examples specific to any audience.

Inspiration in Language Arts
Standards-aligned lesson plans
Improve language arts outcomes with these 30+ standards-based lesson plans covering analysis, persuasion, narration and expression for grades 6-12. Many lessons such as "Literary Comparison" can be used again with different content.

Single book $39.95

Convenient, ready-to-use templates for a variety of lessons are available online at www.inspiration.com.

Achieving Standards with Inspiration 7
Curriculum-aligned lessons for inspired learning
Teachers get started using Inspiration effectively with this set of 35 lesson plans for middle and high schoolers in language arts, social studies and science.

Single book $29.95

Kidspiration in the Classroom
Standards-aligned lesson plans
Effectively integrate Kidspiration 2 with 32 lesson plans in reading and writing, social studies, science and math. Lessons are designed for grades K-2 and 3-5 and include "Writing for an Audience," "Birds of Our School" and "Visualizing Story Problems."

Single book $29.95

Interactive Training CDs
Step-by-step instruction at your own pace

Our interactive, narrated training CDs introduce you to the world of Kidspiration, Inspiration and visual learning. This popular multimedia format lets you learn when your schedule permits—at your own pace. Follow along through the complete step-by-step training or jump to a particular topic or practical classroom example.

Use the CD for individual training, to supplement your in-service training sessions, or for ready reference about specific Kidspiration or Inspiration features and functions.

What's included?
- Visual learning methodologies
- Narrated step-by-step tutorial
- Curriculum-specific examples

Enhanced support for emerging classroom technologies!

Inspiration 7.6 now offers more access to the power of visual learning. Enhanced support for emerging technologies lets students draw symbols and write text directly on interactive electronic whiteboards and Tablet PCs.

NEW!

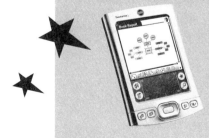

Inspiration® for Palm OS® combines the learning benefits of Inspiration with the natural ease of handhelds. Syncs with Inspiration and Kidspiration® on the desktop. (Single unit $29.95)

Want to share these great lesson plans?

Special Volume Pricing

Now it is easy and cost-effective to assure you are getting the most out of Kidspiration®, Inspiration® and visual learning within your school or across your district. Our standards-based lesson plans help teachers take advantage of the power of visual learning and improve achievement across language arts, science and social studies.

NEW!

Electronic Format

All of our lesson plan books are now available in an easy-to-share electronic format. When you purchase a volume license, you receive a bound copy of the lesson plan book and a CD-ROM version. The CD-ROM includes an Adobe® PDF file of the lesson plan book and ready-for-use templates that support many of the lessons. Simply place the files onto your server to make the lessons instantly available to your staff.

Pricing:

For any single lesson plan book

School-wide license $199

District-wide license $139* (per school licensed)

* Discounts are available when purchasing multiple titles.

ORDER NOW!

Call 800-877-4292 or contact your favorite education software dealer.

Volume licenses available for the following books:

- Kidspiration in the Classroom

- Achieving Standards with Inspiration 7

- Inspiration in Language Arts

- Inspiration in Science

(For more information on these books, see page 110)

7412 SW Beaverton Hillsdale Hwy, Ste 102
Portland, OR 97225-2167 USA

Phone: 503-297-3004
Fax: 503-297-4676
www.inspiration.com